Mrs. Loris Sheets
2151 Pine Canyon Rd
Tooele, UT 84074-9441

MW00677650

To: my Sister of the road —
Lets help each other
always.

Loris a. Sheets

Thank you for sharing
Your time with me.

Sisters of the Road

Sisters of the Road

Stories of Homeless Women in America

Loris Hanson Sheets

1999
Pine Canyon Press
Lincoln, Utah

Library of Congress Cataloging-in-Publication Data
Sheets, Loris Hanson, 1940-
Sisters of the road : stories of homeless women / Loris Hanson Sheets /
p. cm.
ISBN 0-9664795-3-X (hard)
ISBN 0-9664795-0-5 (paper)
1. Homeless women—United States—Biography. 2. Homelessness—
United States—Case studies. I. Title.
HV4505.S55 1998
362.5'082'0973—dc21 98-30112
CIP

Efforts were made to contact all authors (or their representatives) of quotations or words from songs included in the pages of this book. If any were missed, apologies are offered and, upon notification, the omission will be rectified in any subsequent edition of this work.
The quotation from Maya Angelou, *I Know Why the Caged Bird Sings* (copyright © 1969 by Maya Angelou) was reprinted by permission of Random House, Inc.

For my Mother, Doris Goodwin Hanson.
I hope you've found a home in heaven.
You are with me always.
Mother, rest in peace.
Your earthly duties are complete.
Memories remain.

ACKNOWLEDGMENTS

Grateful acknowledgment and appreciation are extended to the following people:

I humbly say thank you to the ladies I interviewed for sharing their lives with us.

To the many social workers, shelter directors and staffs, clergy, employees at soup kitchens, policemen on the streets, and all who contributed in any way to make it possible for me to complete *Sisters of the Road*.

To Richard Firmage for the final editing, design, and production of this book. I will forever be thankful for your knowledge, kindness, and the time you spent on my behalf.

To Jonathan Hinckley and others at Franklin Covey/Publishers Press for helping me achieve my lifelong dream.

To Diane Hamilton Zimmerman and Debra Botte for helpful insight and suggestions.

To Chris Dake for picture graphics and Connie Mayhew for photographs.

To Carol Merrill, counselor at Weber State University, and Gary Acevedo for sharing thoughts and understanding about homelessness and teaching people how to transform their lives.

To Edwin K. (Butch) Dymock, Director, Tooele County Aging and Adult Services, for guidance and support during our years of bringing low-income public housing to our county.

To my parents, both gone now, and my sisters Lorraine, Lorine, Beverly, and our brother, Richard.

To my husband, Ed, with love, appreciation, and great admiration for being an example of dedication in achieving goals, for offering daily encouragement, for being there to support me, and for graciously accepting the job of proof-reading.

To my daughter, Allison Kathleen, and son-in-law Tom Turner. Thank you for your computer and accounting help and your tremendous work ethic. And thank you for sharing with me Stephanie, Gregory, and twins Zachary and Jordan—my loving grandchildren.

To my son, Paul E. Frailey, for building my computer and assembling the system, your knowledge in many things, repeated house calls, and for your wit and laughter—they fixed everything. Thank you for giving me my granddaughter Lauren and her wonderful mother, Tracy.

To my fantastic twin sisters, Lorine Murtagh and Lorraine Shumway. Lorine traveled the U.S.A. with me and encountered all sorts of interesting and dangerous situations. She cleaned shelters and tended children so the ladies could be interviewed; was stopped and held hostage by suspicious citizens; ran for her life from places we hadn't known were off-limits; searched under bridges, in abandoned buildings, railroad cars, boats, banks of rivers, parks, shelters, hospitals, jails, alleys, slum areas, and took pictures of it all (if we weren't running)! Thanks for braving storms, insults, exorcisms, waiting, and waiting some more, and loving every minute of it!

Lorraine also traveled with us on searches for our homeless sisters. Thank you for the compassion you showed the homeless ladies during interviews. Your jokes, singing, and dancing brightened their day. Thank you for your optimism, your talents, your humor, your beliefs and hope, and for your courage.

To my nieces and nephews and their partners: Kelly Cummins, Marty Cummins, Susan Vance Kennedy, who helped arrange interviews at shelters on the east coast, James David Kennedy, Brett Shumway, Karen Gebbie, Mary Martin, Don Martin, Jennifer Robinson, Lacey Manzo, and Shane Stevens. I love our celebrations and get-togethers! Thanks for your hospitality during our travels!

To my cousin, Dr. David Goodwin, and his wife, Jenenne, with respect; both are saviors of lost souls and youth of the world. Your kind hearts have always known what you were meant to do.

To Toby Rice, who shared the driving responsibilities across this big country. She is a compassionate lady who's driven a school bus for handicapped children in Virginia for the past twenty-eight years.

To my old friend, Kathy Koseki Terashima, and her husband, Paul, and family. Thanks for the laughter! Remembering Joe and Ada, always.

To the Smith family—Naomi, Dollie, Don, Judee, and Ronda—for the inspiration you have provided me.

To all the friends, neighbors, and family who nourished my soul during the writing of this book and kept me going. I sincerely appreciated every kind word and deed. I will not try to name you all for fear of leaving someone out in a "senior moment"; but you have inspired me with your courage, lifted me with your kindness, brightened me with your laughter. Thank you all—you know who you are. This book reflects a part of all of you, because you have helped me understand what it means to truly have a home. I couldn't have done my work without you. I apologize for my shortcomings and for any and all mistakes in this book or others yet to be made in my life.

Thank you all from the bottom of my heart.

Contents

Introduction ===================

I BEGAN TO LEARN about the many different kinds of homelessness women face who live in the United States of America during the years I served as a county Public Housing Manager for the U.S. Department of Housing and Urban Development (HUD) in a geographically large county of northwestern Utah. There are helpless, hopeless, depressed, lonely women—many paralyzed by anxiety and fear, ashamed and desperate—wandering the streets and roads looking for a rescue from their nightmare. Over the years, I've interviewed hundreds of homeless women, and I was shocked at the number of "displaced, misplaced, out of place, replaced, with no-place" women who needed help with housing. I also was amazed how quickly some had found themselves without a home. Homeless women are often much the same as you or I; if we had experienced the same set of circumstances and made similar choices in our lives we too might well share their situation. Each woman usually realizes she is down, but she doesn't know quite how or where to turn for support. She is falling without a safety net. Many feel worthless and incapable of escaping their situation, but it is my belief that all deserve our respect and understanding.

Day after day, homeless people came through the office door of the Housing Authority, only to be told that all the housing assistance certificates allocated by the government for our area had been taken and that our waiting lists were long. In short, there was no immediate help for them. Most of the homeless folks were dispirited, and many were full of panic and anxiety when they learned we couldn't help them. The staff assisted them with their applications and promised to contact them as soon as certificates became available. What was espe-

11

cially alarming to me was that many of the women who came were all alone, had no dependent children living at home, were not handicapped or disabled, and weren't fifty-five years of age or older; so we had to tell them they didn't qualify for government housing. Since I fit the requirements of this same category, other than the fact that I wasn't homeless, I paid particular attention to the cold, hard facts of the program and singled out this group, in particular, for study.

The reality that there was no help from the government for some women was hard for me to accept. Some of those affected didn't take the news very well either. When people are desperate, they may well do desperate things. I was threatened with a gun on two occasions, a knife was brandished about my face, a pick of sorts was introduced by one half-crazed man who threatened to use it in an innovative operation on my person, and serious threats were vehemently shouted at me by a few distraught applicants. I was stalked, and threatening notes were left on my desk stating different demands for help; but local social workers seemed to receive more threats and actions against them than those in our office did. I vividly remember an afternoon of a stand-off between the sheriff's department and a woman armed with a shotgun who was beyond the realm of reason because the state had removed her children from her home. Another time, a woman on our housing program was in direct violation of several regulations, and, to avoid eviction and prosecution, hid one child in a large clothes dryer (we found the little girl because she took a puppy into the dryer with her and the animal was whimpering); two other children were hidden in a crawl space under the house.

On several occasions our car tires were flattened, power switches on our breaker boxes were switched off, phone cords were pulled out of the walls, hate mail was received; and verbal assaults were constantly directed our way. We figured it was part of the territory involved in working in the social service field and not being able to offer immediate assistance. The people who had turned violent out of desperation included a young, terminally ill artist whose work had been exhibited in many famous places but who became penniless as a result of high medical costs; a successful businessman who had been cheated out of his fortune and had fallen on hard times; another upstanding citizen who was also terminally ill and needed medication she couldn't afford; an out-of-work family man who'd lived for months in a camper shell with his wife and seven children; and others who were also down on their luck. It is very understandable to me that they acted out of desperation.

Collectively, the government workers made a concentrated effort to help people in need. If local, state, and federal agencies couldn't help, we contacted different religious denominations in the area, thrift stores, various organizations, and people we knew to be "good Samaritans." Finally, if all else failed, we suggested to those in immediate need that maybe they would be better served to leave our area and go where there were more opportunities available to them until we could reach them on the waiting lists.

Over time, the county applied for and received additional housing certificates, built three public housing family projects and several senior citizens housing projects. With the additional units, we were able to house many more people who desperately needed a place to live. When people have a roof over their heads, they can begin to rebuild their lives. It was the common goal of both the Housing Authority and the State Division of Social Services, however, to make services available only as a temporary aid and to encourage tenants of such projects to become self-sufficient, if they were able, and not make assistance programs a way of life. On a brighter side, there are many women working in our county today who were once on assistance programs themselves and who now head or serve in organizations helping women in crisis. These women now live in the best homes in the county—their own.

The county organizations in the area networked closely and were able to help people needing specialized assistance, such as mental health treatment, abuse counseling, shelter, fellowshipping, medication, senior-citizen needs, transportation, vocational training, food delivery, legal help, and direction. It was not uncommon for employees of the support systems to band together during times when tenants who lived alone in the area suffered a loss or tragedy. These workers made hospital visits, provided legal help, went to funerals, gave eulogies, organized fundraisers, provided music, attended services, and in other ways supported their fellow citizens. I cannot praise enough the employees and volunteers of the county organizations who go the extra mile for the less fortunate. I often think of words penned by *Salt Lake Tribune* columnist Robert Kirby: "In the Bible, Christ spared the poor, the sick and even some big-time sinners from his wrath, but he really ripped people who held themselves as more important to God than the less fortunate. We need to think about that more than we do. Things might get a little warm if we don't."

It's a matter of hands. The sisters can only exist from day to day if their hands gather the bare essentials for survival; those same hands must open doors to organizations and agencies where tools for change and opportunity are made available to them. As Robert Kirby suggests, the hearts of the more fortunate must be open and their hands willing to help.

As mentioned, I found myself wanting to study the problems of homeless women. Most of us have recognized some of the faces of homelessness on the streets, but others often are not noticed. The unseen homeless individuals are often trying to blend into the general public, yet they are everywhere. Some still have at least a semblance if not a great deal of pride remaining. More-visible homeless women— sisters of the road, I call them—have usually been on the streets for so long that they are at a point of desperation and uncaring and don't try to hide. These women are very much out in the open as they sometimes literally as well as figuratively beg and cry out, "Help me!" Each homeless woman has a different story; but yet they are often similar to those of others who share the streets.

There are many different faces of homelessness. I remember one occasion when a supervisor in the Tooele County Social Services Department who was also the chairman of the local housing board of directors came to my office and informed me that we had a problem in the county requiring immediate attention. The county covers a very large area, and about forty miles out in a remote rural section was an eighty-year-old woman living alone who needed a place in town to live before winter arrived. The trouble was, although a suitable housing project was under construction, it wasn't ready for occupancy. This particular supervisor always found a way to help his "everyday people," as he called them—it didn't matter how big the obstacles were. The new project included a duplex with a unit for elderly or handicapped people that would meet the needs of the woman, but she would have to be housed elsewhere temporarily. She was the last known surviving member of a family that had practiced polygamy, having outlived both her mother and sister. After polygamy was officially abandoned by the Church of Jesus Christ of Latter-day Saints (Mormons) at the turn of the century, her father reportedly had left her mother, her sister, and herself and returned to his original wife and family.

The rejected family members were resourceful, and, being some-what bitter about the rejection, were further motivated. The women would show the world that they could make it on their own; and, in-deed, they did. The sisters helped their mother with chores needed for their survival and also found time to attend school. Their grades were excellent, and, after graduating from high school, the sisters decided they wanted a college education. But the little family could not send both girls away; the costs for room and board, books, and other living expenses were prohibitive, and their mother needed them at home to help her. The girls enrolled in correspondence courses, however. Many skills also were learned by working outside the home when opportu-nities arose.

The girls never married, and so the household of strong women continued throughout several decades. They managed to put together a small family trust, saving their money when they could, hoping it would sustain them throughout their lives. They lived frugally and kept meticulous financial records. The women were always busy and persevered through many hardships. They managed throughout the years, but old age eventually overtook the women, and the mother and one daughter passed away, leaving the last survivor.

This surviving family member was very independent, believing herself to be totally self-sufficient and still capable of carrying on alone. Her home was badly in need of painting and other repairs and lacked most modern conveniences. The wood-burning stove was used for heat in the winter and also for daily cooking and heating of water for cleaning and other purposes. To make matters worse, this little lady used a wheelchair, making it impossible for her to do the necessary tasks during the harsh winter months that lay just ahead. She had a few kind neighbors who helped considerably with her needs, but it was the assessment of the social service people that she needed to be closer to the medical facilities in town and live in a more controlled environment. The biggest difficulty was persuading her to leave her home. She had always refused help from the government because, as she said, "others need the help more than I do." With great diplomacy and caring, the supervisor from social services proposed a plan. Back and forth they went. Pros. Cons. Debate. Rejection. More talk. More rejection. Questions. Answers. Finally, she agreed to move into town. I'm sure the supervisor used powers he never knew he had; however, there was another big problem. The cost for housing her in town, even temporarily, far exceeded her budget, so creative financing had to be put into play. Somehow, the supervisor saw to it that she was taken care of until the housing project was ready for her to move into. There are angels among us.

When she finally moved into her new apartment at the project, she moved in everything—all her possessions, a new attitude, and a plan for contributing as much as she could to the betterment of the project. She bloomed in her new surroundings, making friends with the little children—teaching them about work, being useful, planting flowers, and playing the old antique chord organ she cherished. She taught the children about saving their pennies and using their heads for knowledge, "not to be a place to store junk and promote a smart aleck attitude." She shared her common sense with the young mothers in the project, explaining to them how to get ahead by working. Her apartment was a hub of activity. She was a regular at her church, submitted articles to the local newspaper about current events, had get-togethers with others interested in history, and taught all who would listen about the rewards of hard work. Her place held treasures. Books of all kinds—especially history books—were everywhere. Keepsakes and other collectibles were displayed and shown to interested visitors. She was an amazing woman who will always be an inspiration to me. This woman could well have been homeless. Hers is one of the many faces of homelessness.

We all rapidly reach the age that makes us an "elderly person." As the years fly by, we're members of that class before we know it. If we've prepared financially and are prepared emotionally, I believe it can be one of the best times in our lives. If a woman has her basic health, a good sense of self, financial security, optimism, and vision to see a bigger picture with purpose and goals not only for herself but for her posterity, she can enjoy her life and make a real contribution in the lives of others.

I have great respect for women who have climbed out of great tragedies during the decades of their lives. I remember helping one little eighty-two-year-old woman fill out some paperwork, and she told me that she had, indeed, had many unhappy and tragic times in her life that she could remember, but that she preferred to forget them. In her own words, "I don't want to burden any of my posterity with troubles that I had—my shoulders were broad, and I could take it." When I visited these older women on government housing programs, either for inspections, contract signings, or renewals, they always had their apartments or homes in spotless condition. Each woman protected her contract by ensuring she met the requirements of both her landlord and the housing authority. Great care was given to everything in her home. Not only did she protect the quarters the government had provided her, she also took great care to protect every item she owned. Her family pictures, handmade knitted and crocheted pillows and throws, and gifts of all kinds from children and grandchildren were treasured and well kept. There was often a grandchild or two visiting, and these grandmothers knew they were loved. Many of them told me that they had taught their granddaughters to knit, bake, cook, bottle fruit and vegetables, and to have respect for others. Grandparents are the link to generations that have gone on before, and impart their knowledge of many things to their young grandchildren. This seems to me to be vital to our civilization, and no amount of money can buy this kind of wisdom and time shared between the generations. In many cases, the elderly are the only people who take time to listen to the children.

Recalling the tenants on the housing programs brings back many wonderful memories. I remember one man of about seventy-five years of age who always walked everywhere he went. He was noticed in our town because of it. He would walk up to six miles on his route to meals at his favorite restaurant and to the homes of friends and family. I remember my first inspection visit to his apartment. He invited me in, and I immediately noticed that it was very clean. The furniture was sparse—just the basic pieces needed for living. He was melancholy as he showed me pictures he had placed on a bookcase. I saw a large picture on one wall that I believed to be of him. "No ma'am," he said, "that's a picture of my twin brother who was hit and killed by a railroad train when he was just seventeen years old. I've missed him every minute of my life since it happened. Our family couldn't understand why it had happened. Maybe he was just hitching a short ride or something like that. It's true that some broken hearts never mend. I know mine hasn't." A person never knows what another is going through as each tries to make it through their days and nights. This man received only a small social security check each month, not enough to rent an apartment, eat, and pay his other living expenses. Without a government housing subsidy, he would have been another face of homelessness.

One lady fixed little cakes and tea for my inspection visits. Her grown son, who was about forty-five years old, lived with her. He was handicapped and used a wheelchair to get around. She doted on him, taking exceptionally good care to see that all his needs were met. Both she and her son each month received a small social security check that didn't even come close to meeting their bills. Every time I came to inspect their apartment, she'd have her beautiful dancing dresses from the 1940s laid out for me to see. She showed me pictures of herself during her party days, and I could see that she had been a very good-looking young woman. Her hometown was Chicago, where she had attended gala parties on nights when the "big bands" played. I saw pictures of her on the dance floors and in booths at the large hotels in town, being romanced by the dapper partners who had escorted her. She claimed to have danced all night on many occasions, and I don't doubt her word. She had saved all the fancy shoes that matched her dresses, and her dance programs still remained of those nights gone by. As she twirled around the floor in front of me, she laughed and laughed, as did her son, and she dreamed . . .

Another elderly woman told me that she'd been orphaned when she was a baby and that her grandmother had raised her. She said, "I adored her and followed right behind her everywhere she went. She was always so kind and loving to me. Wherever grandma went, I went. She was the only mother I ever knew, and I loved her dearly. When I was sixteen years old, she got sick. I was so worried. I remember her asking me for a cool glass of milk, which I brought her. She drank the milk and asked me to turn her on her left side so she would feel a little better, and at that very moment she passed away. It was the first real grief I had experienced. I was sitting by her side when she left this world. Morticians were unheard of in those days, so I combed her hair, knowing it was the last thing I could do for her." It is stories like this that have helped make me realize just how hard a lot of lives are in this old world, and also how much I love being around elderly people. The lady in this story would have been homeless without outside assistance. She received only a small social security check each month, which wasn't even enough to pay the rent.

I have dozens of stories from my experiences with the government housing program. There are tragedies that many probably wouldn't believe, and there also are stories that warm the heart. One man who was in the housing program was known in our town for "tipping the bottle," and I was leery to go to his apartment for an inspection. I remember cautiously knocking on his door; but, when it opened, I was stunned as I looked past the man and saw the beautiful interior. He invited me in, and I noticed his diplomas from prestigious universities along with many framed letters of commendation, honors, and patents. He was an inventor and a decorated veteran of World War II. I was very impressed by the real man and ashamed of my preconceived notions—a lesson I tell here, as I have tried to remember it when I meet homeless people, reminding myself not to pre-judge anyone. I also believe that as long as a person shows prejudice and believes the world is full of misfits, fear, and danger, the world will be that way for them. Family troubles had brought him to other problems; but there is no doubt that this man had much to offer those who would give him the opportunity.

During the years I worked with homeless people, I had the good fortune of working with various agencies and organizations involved with outreach programs and missions in the areas where homeless men and women stayed. They offered help by attending to medical needs and by providing food, clothing, housing, jobs, rehabilitation of one kind or another, and many other services. These outreach groups found homeless people living in some of the strangest places: structures that were substandard or abandoned, hiding places where homeless individuals felt some degree of safety and privacy, and places where large numbers congregated, such as parks. Some homeless people didn't want to be found.

I've felt welcome around most homeless people; but there were those who weren't happy to see or speak to us. It didn't seem to matter to most, though, that we arrived unexpectedly and intruded in their space. They always preferred an orange crate, tree stump, barrel, or somewhere for us to sit. Men generally had a special box or bag with such items as their military dog tags, various papers, medals, pictures, cigarettes and lighters, matches, and maybe a weapon of sorts. Some told their story; others didn't speak at all. Some had Bibles; others had girlie magazines. Women usually had carts or bags full of their clothing and personal items. I can't remember seeing any purses. Many homeless people cried when they told their stories. A few offered to share what little food or drink they had. If a Veterans Administration Hospital was located nearby, an outreach medical assistance team usually was in the area to help military veterans. Aid stations from other organizations offered many kinds of assistance. These stations often were set up under overpasses, near bridges and viaducts, in parks, around shelters and soup kitchens, and at other places where homeless men and women gather. There is a lot of good being done by some people in this country.

Housewives are among the many faces of homelessness. In fact, their numbers are claimed to be higher than those of any other group. Many women are brought to housing agencies by family members; some have no transportation of their own, while others have never driven a vehicle. Not learning to drive wasn't uncommon in earlier generations, and neither was staying at home and not working in the outside world. Most girls married soon after their high school graduation. Many lived fulfilling lives as housewives and mothers, hoping to live "happily ever after" in that role. Unfortunately, however, often unpleasant events happen and circumstances change. If a woman is fortunate, she will have the means to sustain herself and her children should her partner die or leave. With careful planning, adequate insurance policies and survivor benefits can ensure the security the family will need to survive. Other women, however, find out that after the loss of a partner they have insufficient income to pay the bills each month. A common thread I found running through their stories was that some hadn't taken sufficient financial steps to ensure that a home would always be there for them. If a woman does not own her own home, or if the home is not paid for and there is insufficient insurance to pay it off, she may not be able to afford the home and will be forced to sell it and rent a place elsewhere. Renting at current market rates might be more than she can afford. Without education beyond high school or a marketable skill learned along the way, her housing budget might be inadequate to meet housing costs. There probably are millions of women in this country who are in this particular situation. Without a support system of some kind, whether it be family, government, church, friends, or some other source, these women will become homeless. Some homeless women told me that in order to avoid this situation they remarried soon, often with harmful consequences; others said that they prostituted themselves in order to avoid living on the streets.

Even though housewives are hardworking women and have worked alongside other family members their entire lives, they do not receive monetary payments for their work, nor have they paid into private or government retirement systems. If they can show no record of contribution, there will be no payments due them, except maybe a small survivor benefit from their husband's social security contributions or pension. Another drawback to their situation is never having established any credit in their own name, which often results in them not being able to obtain credit from banks or other lending institutions.

Many of the women who come to the government for help don't qualify for assistance. Even though the women have homelessness in common, some find themselves disqualified because they, as I've stated before and want to reinforce, have no dependent children living with them, are not disabled or handicapped, and are not over fifty-five years of age. If women work at even a minimum-wage job, it can disqualify them for assistance from state and federal programs, and they may even be disqualified for schooling or training assistance. This policy may not be fair, but those are the rules that must be followed. I believe that women who do fall through the cracks in the system constitute the greatest number of homeless women; but most of them exhaust all other sources of help before being reduced to this situation.

I would like to quote from a letter written to an Ogden, Utah, newspaper by one homeless woman:

> The fact is that you [as a homeless woman] don't qualify for much of anything, except being somebody's live-in bimbo, provided you can cook and do laundry, so why don't you crawl in some hole and stop wasting everybody's time? How long can you live in fear and terror and trauma, getting poor nutrition and going it alone, with no support and everything going against you, before something gives? My last marriage ended when I would no longer compromise my beliefs. I had to fight for my life as an individual and as a human being worth something, or die a slow death in bondage to other people and a lifestyle that had never been even close to what I wanted....
>
> I lost my home, two cars, all my "friends" and most of my family. I spend a lot of time on the streets and on the bus. The abuse and degradation I have suffered has not come from street people. It comes from people who "assume" too much; who assume that I am gutter trash. Well, if gutter trash is something that has been thrown out because no one has any use for it, then maybe I am.

There are all kinds of people in all walks of life, and the different classifications are not indicative of street people. There are snot-nosed arrogant liars, thieves, alcoholics, drug addicts, child molesters, and ignorant abusive people everywhere. But it's just easier to hide what you "are" behind what you "have" and pretend to be. There is humility born in the despair which we prostitute ourselves to avoid. I am somebody, and I have survived against odds the majority of society would do anything to avoid being subjected to, and I at least can look at myself in the mirror.

To me, those are words of wisdom. I promised myself that when I retired from federal service and had time to work toward improving programs involving homelessness I would find a way to inform as many people as I could about the plight of homeless women. I would have time to travel and interview them and learn more about what causes this national tragedy. Writing this book is my way of keeping the promise I made to myself. If the words I've written help make any reader care and take some action, I won't have wasted the printer's ink.

I've spoken to many women living on the streets, hoping to learn more about the reasons for their condition or, in the case of some, their lifestyle. I chanced to meet one homeless woman at a park in the Phoenix, Arizona, area early one evening before the blackness of night fell upon us. She sat alone on a park bench, talking out loud to an invisible being. She seemed to be trying to remember a song from her childhood. "Momma, tell me the words again that you and I used to sing from our songbook when I was little," she said, speaking in a childlike voice. Slowly, she remembered some words and haltingly sang, "I help Mother with the dishes, just as often as she wishes ... by and by, when I am grown, I'll do dishes all alone." The woman suddenly became very animated, seeming to be both disgusted and angry at herself. She didn't seem satisfied with the way she had sung the song, and shouted, "No, that wasn't the way it went at all! There were more words. I don't want to do dishes all alone!" Suddenly, she jumped off the bench and wheeled her shopping cart toward me, still talking to herself. She screamed at me, "I'm all grown up now, but I have no dishes and no sink, and no mother, either. What happened to them?" I spoke to her briefly before she walked away, recognizing that she was both mentally and physically impaired. She mimicked me as I spoke to her. I watched her and other people leave the park as the lights of the city came on. I believe outreach programs should bring homeless women with serious mental and physical problems to facilities where they can be properly cared for on a permanent basis.

Not all weather in our country is as warm as it is in Arizona, and homeless people have an extra burden to bear in cold climates. Within a few hours after I arrived in Chicago during a horrible snowstorm one winter, I met some street people who weren't faring so well. The cold wind blowing off Lake Michigan was chilling everyone in its path. As I walked on the north side of town, heading toward an overnight women's shelter, I noticed a woman and her two small children sheltering under a big cardboard box in an alley. She yelled to me, "Excuse me, lady, do you know where there's a thrift store?" When I got closer to her, she said, "I need to get some warm coats for my kids and myself before nightfall, and, if I'm lucky, no one will steal them from us tonight like they did last night. I begged the thief, 'please, don't hurt us! Let us stay warm.' Imagine, someone stealing our coats, things we really need. He didn't need those coats. He already had one, and probably traded our coats for drugs. That devil came out in the cold! Lady, my eyes plead with those who pass by, but they just turn away. If they don't think I'm capable of putting their gifts to good use, I wish they'd give them to my children.... I keep on the move so social services won't take my kids away from me. I can't keep them in school when we don't have a home."

I asked her, "Where did you sleep last night?" "You don't want to know, nor do I want to tell you," she answered. I promised to send someone to help them. As I walked away, I pondered many things. I'd always thought that childhood was such an amazing time and had never wanted it to end. How did these children feel about their childhood? I tried not to think of how they looked. Why had the woman and her children stayed on the streets instead of at the family shelter on Marine Lake? Maybe it had been full, or maybe she thought the social workers might take her children away from her because of their living conditions.

I hadn't walked very far up the street when I noticed an elderly woman lying alone on a large piece of cardboard. She was fully dressed in a long coat, boots, and gloves. Beside her, next to her head, were her false teeth and a can of pork and beans with a plastic spoon in the can. Her long gray hair partially hid her face and some of it was frozen in the beans. What a sad sight to see. There was snow all around her. I touched her to make sure she was alive, and she stirred. I asked if she felt like walking to the shelter with me. She replied, "Go away and leave me alone." I told her I would send someone to help her, and could only wonder why she too wasn't staying at a shelter. It wasn't that far away, and she was apparently alone.

I walked to the Salvation Army's overnight women's shelter and told them about those I'd seen on the street. The man at the front desk said, "We will outreach them. God bless you." He promised to send someone out to locate them. The Salvation Army does so much for the homeless. Please, don't ever walk past one of their bell-ringers without contributing something. Just don't.

After checking out of the hotel where I stayed in Chicago, I seated myself in the lobby for a while before catching my airline flight back home. A smartly dressed woman soon approached me. "Can you tell me what time it is?" she asked. I told her the time and then recalled that I'd seen her serving herself earlier at a buffet table where a luncheon was being served by a national organization hosting a convention. Our conversation continued, and she asked me what I was doing in Chicago. I told her that I was interviewing homeless women. She laughed nervously and said, "I guess I'm a homeless woman."

"Are you kidding?" I asked her.

This very distinguished-looking lady told me that she was an unemployed stock broker who was trying to survive until she could find another job. She continued, "Most of the single business women I know live from payday to payday. Maybe there won't be a payday for me for a while; but I don't even want to visit that idea." She related that things were going well for her after her graduation from college and that she later received a broker's license. However, her firm downsized. "Being very proud, and not wanting to return to the small town where everyone believed me to be a success, I remained here in Chicago trying to do my best to survive," she continued. "I've depleted my savings account, my apartment lease was not renewed, my BMW was repossessed, and I've sold most of my clothing and all of my jewelry, including my watch." She was too proud to ask anyone she knew for money or help, but she did lie to them in order to obtain some help. Now, at this stage of homelessness, she was doing "creative gathering of food and practicing some vagrancy evasion tactics to survive. I read used newspapers to locate events serving free food, such as wedding receptions, conventions, happy hours, stores serving food samples, church socials, funeral dinners, and any other means I can conceive of to get me through each day."

She sold her blood and said she had even been used as a "guinea pig" for a large pharmaceutical company in a research project. She either walked or asked strangers for rides to business interviews and said she once walked seventeen miles in high-heel shoes to an interview. "I clean up and wash my clothes in the restrooms of hospitals, bus and train stations, airports, stores, restaurants, hotels, and even at a mortuary one night during the viewing hours of a total stranger, claiming she was an old friend. I figured the poor woman couldn't deny it. I've slept in bushes on the grounds of first-class hotels or anywhere else I could find that was inconspicuous and as safe as possible," she confessed to me. I suggested she go back home to regroup and gather herself. Her parents had no idea she had lost her job and was in trouble. I told her that there was no disgrace in losing a job due to downsizing, but losing her life on the streets and causing that kind of grief to her family and friends would be a real tragedy. I still often wonder what happened to that lady. Another face of homelessness.

The brief stories of these homeless women that I've just shared with you are very different but yet similar in some respects, particularly as abrupt or gradual developments reveal a person's vulnerability. Each one of us would do well to realize that we could end up homeless if we should lose our means of support and self-sufficiency.

I've spoken to a lot of women walking city sidewalks at night. Many complained that they were too cold, too hungry, or too tired to keep up the nonstop motion of their steps leading them nowhere, just so they could keep from freezing to death. Maybe those tired ones found the strength to find a shelter that wasn't filled to capacity. Maybe they were able to find a bus station or a church where the police or security people didn't chase them away for vagrancy. Maybe they weren't so lucky. Many homeless women die of exposure.

What do the women in these stories have in common? One answer is simple: they have no "home." The dictionary defines home as a "place where something or someone is naturally found." I believe this to mean a place where one belongs. Being "homeless" is defined as "having no home." A home is a place where a woman can be herself, and, if lucky, will be accepted as she is. It is a place where she can grow, can discover who she is and learn to like herself; it is a place where she can study, read, play, rest, heal and renew herself, laugh, pray, learn values, and give thanks for the blessing of having a home and all that's in it. A home is a refuge from the world.

A home isn't any particular structure. A shack may be more a home than is a mansion on a hill; but most people need the protection and assurance of a secure and stable refuge, a substantial structure to shelter them. To have a home usually means that someone has made a sacrifice to purchase or acquire it. A home should not be taken for granted. It is a place from which we venture and a place to which we can return. A home is a place where we can start from to accomplish our life's work and goals, and a place to return if we fail, or to seek forgiveness after doing wrong. It is a place where, hopefully, we can feel loved.

Home is a place where we can keep things that are important to us—food, health products, furnishings, vehicles, legal documents, private papers, clothes, personal items, musical instruments, remembrances, and awards. It is a place where we can develop our talents and polish our manners. It is a gathering place for our family, friends, and pets; it's a place where someone can deliver a valentine card addressed to us; a place where a date can call to take us to a dance; a place where an important letter or surprise package can be delivered with our name on it, where we can receive a telephone call, where the knock at the door will be for us. These things occur in a home. Home is also the place where we nurture our offspring, and where we sit around the dinner table and talk about the events of our day. This same home can protect us from threatening weather, from many dangers, and from the loneliness of the streets.

This book is about women who have lost their homes. Some of them have contributed to the loss; others have lost their homes due to no real fault of their own. Reasons for such loss include illness, fire, floods and other disasters of nature, job loss, abandonment by another, death of a spouse, divorce, crimes committed against or by people, addictions of one kind or another, among many other circumstances and reasons. Some people have lost their homes as a result or a combination of their actions or inactions, their poor judgement in choosing friends or companions, their desires, or their poor financial management skills. Homeless women have relinquished their homes, and many times have handed over much of their power, their independence, and their lives, finally ending up homeless on the streets. Some can be helped back into society. Some cannot.

I was always looking for a common thread that ran through the lives and circumstances of homeless women. I discovered that, in some cases, homeless women had several common strands running through their stories; in other words, similar mistakes were made by them in their lives before they reached the streets. One common thread I found was that many homeless women hadn't taken sufficient financial steps to ensure that a home would always be there for them. Another thread was repeatedly choosing bad companions and friends. I also became acutely aware of another common thread that seemed to bind some of the women together. These women were hanging onto an old paradigm or behavior pattern that cast themselves in the role as pitiful victims. This role had brought them through dozens of tragedies. Many of these women of tragedy seemed to play secondary games, hoping their payoffs would be attention, feelings of much-deserved pity, or rescue by others. Once one assumes this role, it is a hard one to leave. Many women play roles for approval, and, if keeping themselves in the role of a lowly victim is what brings them the most attention, that seems to be enough for them. Other women I talked with were in total denial that they had played any part in reaching their situation as a homeless woman, but their stories revealed otherwise. "I don't know how I became homeless, it just happened," many told me. Without intervention, I'm afraid these women will remain homeless and continue to experience more misery and danger.

I've wondered many times what the essence of homelessness might be. I've deliberated a great deal about the reasons so many women live on the streets. One day I decided to make a chart with categories for each of the reasons given me. It was a reckoning of sorts in an effort to determine the main cause of women being homeless. The facts seemed to be telling me that the reasons many women gave me for being homeless had placed them squarely in what I call the "selfless women" category, using the term in the sense that they had not accepted responsibility for their lives, if they were capable of doing so. Most of them had no plans for their future; some had given up their power to others; some lived their lives in a reckless, careless or wild manner; many were undependable and untrustworthy. A multitude of them thought they would or should be taken care of by someone else.

I've heard a woman cry for half an hour without stopping after I had asked her to tell me about her homelessness. It was heartbreaking to witness her wanting to speak but not being able to. It was hard to watch her enduring the type of misery she was experiencing. I've watched women struggle to stay focused long enough to complete a sentence, to recall events from their past, to remember their birthday, their hometown, how long they've been homeless, or where they slept the night before. Their way of thinking might not be rational, but they often don't see it that way. Their stories might be fragmented, vague, or not in the order they happened. Some may not remember anything about their lives. Others lose their thoughts in mid-sentence and then just stare off into the distance. Some of their thoughts were scattered or fragmented. I'm afraid living on the streets has exacted a heavy toll.

A word is necessary about the stories you are about to read—these are edited transcripts of the actual interviews. For most interviews I carried with me a pocket tape recorder, which I used to record the conversation (gaining the permission of the interviewee in all cases). Some conversations and interviews caught me less prepared, however, and during the course of these I would jot down notes as we talked, amplifying these notes later with my recollections and with those of others who might have accompanied me.

The material in quotes are actual words used by me and the women with whom I talked; however, I have eliminated most of the off-color language, which was very commonly used by some women. Although at times I had second thoughts about this decision, feeling that I have thus lost much of the emotion and harsher reality of the women's lives, I feel that such language can ultimately be a distraction from the basic tale—the telling of which is my primary aim. Therefore, interruptions, outbursts of temper, and other distractions are generally eliminated, although I have tried to establish a bit of the setting of the various interviews and the mood and circumstances of the women at the time of the interview. Repetition was frequent in the tales, and this too has generally been omitted, along with whole digressions, a few of which I summarized.

The reader thus should be aware that this would be a poor sociological or psychological treatise in an academic sense; however, I hope that there are some compensating strengths to the book. By concentrating on the basic story, I hope that it comes into sharper focus, for

I believe that the essential facts are gritty enough to show the heart-ache and danger experienced by these women and to hint at the loss experienced by them, their loved ones, and all of society by their plight on the margins and in the shadows of our social network. I hope that the combination of summarization sprinkled with actual dialogue will bring both immediacy and clarity to the tales. Since it is my ultimate hope to help other women avoid such a plight and to stir others to act to aid those already suffering, this clarity seemed the most important value to me and thus helped form my narrative method.

I do want to assure the reader, however, that I have not taken any liberties to dramatize any of these tales or to manufacture dialogue to make a point. There remains much that will probably perplex many readers, as it still confuses me, in fact. These are real women in a hard social setting, subject to danger, confusion, fatigue, anger, and the rest of the emotions we humans regularly manifest. It is my belief that acts of charity, acts of kindness, and a willingness to listen and not pre-judge may lead to an enrichment of our own lives. These women have much to teach us—both through their situation and in their hearts and minds. Some, as I hope to indicate, revealed to me remarkable love, sacrifice, and endurance; and if only these qualities could be freed from the fetters of their homeless situation, one can imagine how much brighter these people could make our world.

This is not to say that it was always a pleasant task to interview the women. They live in a hard world where it can be a struggle literally to survive from day to day. Most have become very tough, hardened in many ways. These were not casual chats over tea and coffeecake. I'm sure many were wary of me; others probably looked for some kind of immediate gain for their cooperation; others just wanted an ear to hear their laments, to listen to how they had been wronged.

I did not consider it my strength or my task to ask hard questions to verify the actual facts of the stories told; however, I did my best to question the women about certain things they told me to gain a better understanding of the story. Some were incapable of telling the whole truth, possibly in some cases because they couldn't remember much of what had happened to them, or they might fantasize. Maybe they simply didn't want to remember. Some looked to get a response that would make them feel important. Profanity was quite common. Some believed that no one believes a word they say and were paranoid about every word and action taken by others. It was hard to determine some-

times just what to believe; but I don't think that my individual conclu-
sions are that important to this book. Many gifted people can analyze
things in many different ways. The actual tale told—whatever its ultimate veracity—constitutes the basic material of this book.

Most of the women were lonely for companionship and someone
to talk to, so some went on and on just to keep the new company
they'd found. Many homeless women are very intelligent, perhaps
much smarter than you or I. Some perceive themselves as weak and
stupid. They feel they have no value, and they can't find the door out
of low self-esteem and depression—the door that leads to action and
recovery. More than a few became little girls again in the telling of
their stories, because their dreams are there. If only they could return
to the days of their youth—maybe this time around they would better
learn certain lessons.

I ask readers to be patient with the telling as you read the stories.
Most of the women were troubled, and some were not always completely coherent. Some names, places, and identifying details have been
changed to protect the privacy of the women involved. Any photographs used in the book have been altered to protect their identities.

It was an adventure and a great experience for me to meet and
listen to homeless women. Maybe some good will come from reading
their stories. I hope so, and believe that they hope so, too. I'd now like
you to meet Dominique, Cheryl, Saige, Cecily, Jolene, Kathleen, Starr,
Isabelle, Julie, and Sarah—just a few of the women I have met and a
tiny handful of the thousands of homeless women in our nation today. There are so many stories that need telling, and so few pages in
this book. The stories of the following women were chosen because
they are somewhat diverse. Some women wanted their stories told but
wanted to remain anonymous. Others were proud of their recovery
efforts and wanted to share their stories and pictures. I have used
fictitious names and chose not to include full portraits of the women.
One woman suggested I call the book *The Little Helper Book for Homeless Women.* I hope the book is that and more. *The Little Helper Book to
Keep Women from Becoming Homeless* would be a name that I would
like if the book is able to actually serve such a function. For now, I am
pleased to call it *Sisters of the Road,* for I hope that title will indicate
both the plight of these women and their kinship to the rest of us.

Dominique ═══════════

NEW ORLEANS, Louisiana, is an exotic locale; however, I traveled there one spring to visit with homeless women there. Upon my arrival, I decided to take a tour of the city and soon fell in love with the old river parish community. It was home to a real diversity of people who daily practiced their religion, arts and crafts, celebrations, architecture, cooking, and family traditions. Their way of life was deeply ingrained, as is the case with most really great places to live. The exquisite residences, the mild winters, and lively festivals can make living a pleasure in this venerable old city. However, the city also was experiencing growth and change, and some changes breed crime and crowding. Many residents thus were desperately trying to protect their ethnic cultures and traditions. Their message seemed to be, "It's fine to enjoy your visit here, but don't compromise our quality of life."

After taking the tour, I found my way to the historic river region and observed people in the outdoor cafes. The cups of café au lait were steaming and the beignets were sweet and very pleasing to my palate. Crowds were browsing through the shops, restaurants, and gathering places. Artists were gathering, and sounds of accordion and jazz filled the air. Interesting places, it seems, attract the most interesting people. Suddenly, I caught a glimpse of a most unusual object in front of a coffee house and stared at it for several minutes with great curiosity. Leaning against the French window was something wonderful … an arty display of some kind. I couldn't identify the object, and its purpose or function was a complete mystery to me. Finally, I stood up and walked closer for a better look. There were two wheels and a handle; the basic structure was that of an upright cart. Colorful satin ribbons were wrapped tightly around the metal rods. A large pouchlike bag covered with floral tapestries seemed to be filled to capacity. Woven fringed shawls in subdued colors were loosely draped around the bag, as were pieces of soft velvet fabric in deep, rich colors. Carefully pinned to the center of the pouch were a metal cross and a picture of a child in a delicate filigree frame. Two half-burned candles were tied next to them. An umbrella with a handle adorned with objets d'art also hung from the cart, and elastic cords wrapped in satin ribbons held the precious cargo to the cart frame. By these means, the mysterious object presented a shrine-like appearance. I wondered why it was there, and felt like an intruder just looking at it.

Suddenly, the coffee house door was flung open and loud voices were heard arguing over the nonpayment of a purchase. "The tea was absolutely horrible! I cannot swallow another mouthful of such rancid tasting, decaying fluid!" shouted the woman. She was careful to enunciate her words so they had the desired theatrical effect. The woman turned back and yelled, "There's no way I'm going to allow any more of that high-priced poison into my body, let alone pay for it!" The irate customer was exotic looking. I sensed a mystery or secret about her that I believe only wandering gypsies know—maybe it was due in part to the pair of golden coin earrings she wore. I thought of a gypsy story that if you wear a pair of golden earrings love will come to you. I knew immediately she was the owner of the cart. I was in awe of her appearance and the way in which she carried herself. I had just met Dominique, although we hadn't been formally introduced.

The woman moved toward the cart with hurried grace, like an actress or dancer from one of the festivals in town. A wide bright pink-and-black floral headpiece pulled back her black hair, except for a few locks that framed her beautiful, pensive face. Large dark glasses hid the windows to her soul. Her dress of rich black satin was trimmed with bright pink satin ruffles around the neck and bottom of the skirt. A black lace shawl was draped around her shoulders. Several gold chains hung from her neck—some with charms and others with pictures of a young girl at varying ages. The miniature metal coins jingled from her ears as she walked. Her overall look somewhat resembled a Tarantella dancer. She certainly had the thin figure of a dancer. I wanted to know more about this mystical-looking woman who had just fled the coffee house. I was sure the charms on her necklace were connections to her past. I wondered if they were given to her by loved ones or friends.

The irate woman wheeled her cart to the outdoor eating area and stopped. She leaned against a wood railing and stood there for a few moments, alone with her thoughts. I was apprehensive about approaching her for fear she would be angry and cause a scene. She seemed to be feisty and unpredictable; however, I finally decided to approach her. Some people just demand special attention, and I wasn't about to let her slip away without finding out more about her. My curiosity definitely had gotten the best of me.

I walked up to her very cautiously, introduced myself, and said, "I couldn't help but notice you leaving the coffee house. I've already noticed your cart; it's quite unique, very intriguing. I hope you won't take offense to my speaking to you, but, if you're in no hurry, I was wondering if you would like to join me at my table for a few minutes. I can get you something better than rancid tea to drink." As she didn't immediately reply to my comments, I continued, "You have such an interesting dress and manner."

Calmly, without emotion, she said, "I'm a woman who lives alone in the world. My name is Dominique." She nodded her head in the direction of an area across the street and said, "I live over there, past that black wrought-iron gate." I looked beyond the gate into a narrow passageway. Before I could say anything, she continued, "I *live* in that passageway. You can follow me across the street if you'd like and talk with me there. I'm going home. I've had quite enough for one day."

I didn't know why Dominique invited me to join her, but she had, so I followed her across the street, through the gate, and into the passageway. She said, "I'd like a few minutes to gather myself," and seated herself gracefully on an old pine cabinet, almost as though she was posing. She positioned her legs and feet much as a ballet dancer or person with impeccable manners would do, revealing to me an uptown pedigree. As I stood watching her, my thoughts wandered to lines of a song: "What stories, Belle, do your dances tell? After you hide, do you float and glide … on the asphalt that is your stage in your wrought-iron cage?"

The walls of the neighboring buildings were made of old weathered brick. The black wrought-iron gate and fence added to the setting, as did the tall, black iron lamp post just outside on the street. Dominique's fingers gently rubbed the cabinet, and, after a few minutes had passed, her lips curved in a faint smile as she said, "This might not look like much of a home to you, but I've fixed it up so that I love being here. I'm not afraid of my homelessness. See the hanging wrought iron planter over on that wall? My plant does very well there and is happy. 'Bloom where you are' applies to people too, if we can navigate through the weeds and prickly thorns put in our path."

I did not have my tape recorder with me, much to my regret; the unexpected encounter had caught me off guard. I usually carried it— always when I planned or hoped to meet with homeless women— however, I was determined to learn what I could of this intriguing homeless woman who yet seemed to have made a home in the streets.

"I keep my possessions in this cabinet," she explained, as she got down from the cabinet and opened its rustic door with a key that she wore on her necklace. She went on, "See the bottle of buttons I've saved? They were removed from favorite dresses I wore during my childhood and teenage years … days that are gone forever. I wonder whatever happened to all my dresses? My mother always thought it strange of me to save the buttons. Here's my favorite book. I keep my dried flowers pressed between its pages. See how the old Persian carpet covers the asphalt?. . . Someone was kind enough to leave it for me while I was gone one day. It's all so perfect."

Dominique again sat on the cabinet, saying, "Homelessness is a state of mind. There are different kinds of homelessness. A woman can be homeless and not even know it. She can own and occupy the same beautiful house with her husband, but if he has a crafty lawyer and a judge in his pocket, she can be out in the street and homeless in the blink of an eye. You need a reason? She doesn't quite fill the bill any longer. Are mothers and wives really that disposable?" she asked, expecting no answer, as it seemed that she had almost forgotten me as she revealed glimpses of her history in her developing monologue.

"What was I sacrificed for—a mid-life crisis, or a lifestyle that was faster and higher? Why can't a male just tell you that he wants a party doll with tighter buns? I tried to look right for him, and I did what he wanted me to do. Why did he have to destroy me and then leave? Why couldn't he just have been honest with me when he first decided he wanted out … while I still had my health, my wealth, some dignity, and some options? Why was he so cowardly in the deceitful manner in which he left his family?"

She mentioned that her husband had had affairs, but always told her they meant nothing to him. "Didn't he realize that an affair lasts long enough to ruin one's most important relationships?" Dominique appeared to be in a state of reverie and spoke slowly, her words softly echoing in the alley. She spoke bitterly about the breakup of her marriage and the loss of her home. It was obvious that "home" was something that mattered deeply to her, and her words should have been heard by many more ears than mine.

"So many big new homes with their perfect floors and doors and windows sit alone all day long while their owners work to pay for them. No mother, no father, no children in them during the daytime hours; not to mention the nights when they are dark and deserted because the family members are all out becoming strangers to one another. Oh, the poor house pets, too. What happened to them? What happened to the dinners where my family ate together and gathered around our table and talked about their day?" Dominique wondered aloud.

A conversation gradually developed between us, with me gently prodding or quesioning some aspects, while Dominique generally reminisced or recalled events, many of which I tried to piece together later. Still, her account was generally clear and well expressed. Her broken marriage dominated much of her thought.

"Later in my married life I would say to my husband, 'Would you please just speak to me or give me the time of day, maybe send me some flowers?' I felt as if I wasn't really there. Even at that time I wondered if I would have to settle for dead flowers and conversations with myself someday," Dominique said sorrowfully, remembering her suspicions. She continued her story, telling of a darker side of her relationship with her ex-husband. She had alluded to the fact that he was a drug user, and I wondered if he had lured her into that destructive lifestyle also. She confirmed this. "I followed the greedy-eyed piper down alleys to the voodoo land of bad spirits, potions, powders and hooch, mostly. The bad spirits crazed my mind and body, leaving me with nothing but poor memory and aloneness. The potions were mixed—some kind of hallucinogenic potpourri. Maybe a curse was put on me for slipping down the alley … 'come along, or be alone, you'll party with me. For if you don't, and say, "I won't," the worst is yet to be!' Marie Laveau was blamed for giving voodoo a bad name. Well, I think my ex-husband should share the blame. He exploited me and he exploited voodoo."

"Do you know what I mean?" she suddenly asked me, seeming to believe she'd done all that could have been expected of her to save their marriage, but that she still didn't feel good about it.

"I don't really understand what you mean, Dominique," I answered.

"Well, I don't understand either, because I'm no longer my old self … and I'm not familiar with the person I've become who doesn't seem to remember," Dominique said.

"How long have you been homeless?" I asked her in an attempt to get back to more solid ground.

"A long, long time. I no longer keep track of time. I have silence here, but I like this kind of silence. I'm not hiding and it's my choice if I let people find me. The silence and tension were different in my big home—they were my landlords. Rejection and ugliness were my room-mates. You see, I lived with a very self-centered, cruel husband. He did shifty things and changed himself. I should have known what he was up to … the little fast sports car and golden chains, the manicured mustache and monetary gains. There are moments in your life when you realize nothing will ever be the same," Dominique answered, with a sadness in her voice.

"Some people live in heaven through no fault of their own. Yes, someone is in heaven and a mother is in hell," Dominique told me with bitter resignation. Then she stared into space in a type of reverie—as I later noticed she often did—her fingers gently stroking the framed picture on her necklace.

"Who's in heaven?" I asked her.

She answered, "It's not my ex-husband, that's for sure! No, he'll never get to heaven, not him. He embezzled everything I ever had. My dignity. My pride. My health. My family's money. My money. He beat me and killed my children. Money and social position won't get him a place in heaven; believe me, that's all he has and they don't count. He's the one who should have burned! That's enough about him!" she yelled. "I've paid dearly for knowing that slick bastard!"

Having said that, Dominique swayed slightly back and forth and softly began humming, then singing, a Joan Baez song that I happened to know. Its lines included the words, "It's all come back too clearly. Yes, I loved you dearly. And if you're offering me diamonds and rust, I've already paid."

It seemed that Dominique indeed had paid, but I wondered who Dominique was talking about when she said that someone had "burned." She became angry and even had a tendency to scream at the very thought of her ex-husband. It seemed to be almost too painful for her to talk about him. She was always serious as she spoke about her life, but her accounts were fractured and meanings were hard to understand.

Dominique had a hard, persistent cough. I asked her if she'd been examined by a doctor. "Sounds like bronchitis again—I've had it before," she replied. I remonstrated that bronchitis is a very serious illness and that she shouldn't neglect her condition. She replied matter-of-factly, "I've gone to doctors before when I thought I might have pneumonia, but they just gave me prescriptions I didn't need and charged me for them. I don't trust doctors. I've been drugged before. I have no money now, and I don't want others to pay for my care; besides, they'll eventually expect something from me. I think my family might be working with them to put me in a facility of some kind. I don't want this to happen to me as it has before. I'm fine. Just give me some milk and I can get better, but don't add sugar or Valium to it. Food stamps are just a waste for me; just give me the basics—a big sack of flour, some milk, a little butter, a big block of cheese, some citrus fruit for vitamin C, and a little piece of ground where I can grow herbs and vegetables," she explained.

"How are you getting food?" I asked.

"The people who work in the eating establishments around here are very kind to me," Dominique responded. She then told me that on some holidays the restaurant personnel put food for her in baskets adorned with shiny ribbons and appropriate decorations for the particular holiday. She pointed to some baskets that were stacked in a corner.

"Have you tried to get help with your housing needs so you won't have to deal with the dangers of the streets?" I questioned.

Her response surprised me not only by its rejection of the idea but by its vehemence. "I can't think about that or I'll defeat myself, because agencies will just take control of my life and take away my freedom. Not much happens in my life now that isn't on my terms. There are just too many rules and regulations the agencies want me to follow. They want to record everything about me. I want nothing to do with them. Agencies—a perfect name for them, because they just want to take away my free agency. I couldn't continue going on my long walks, and they are what keep me going. The court system saw to it that I lost my nice home and made me homeless. They gave it to my thieving husband, so why would I want to go on any of their housing programs now?" Dominique retorted angrily.

"Say, I was just wondering if you could help me with something?" Dominique asked, after a pause.

"If I can, I surely will," I replied.

After a few moments' hesitation, Dominique asked, "Will you look around this alley on the walls and above the doors to see if you can detect a hidden camera? I know people have been watching me to see what I'm doing. They're spying on me day and night. I thought I'd figured out a way to tell if they were or not, but I'm still not sure. I decided that since I'm always being asked about the different things I do, if they saw me doing something really off-the-wall they would ask me about that too."

She again hesitated; but her need to tell me something outweighed her reluctance. "Well, I'm embarrassed to tell you what I did. I sucked my thumb for a whole day! Surely, I thought, these people who show such great concern for my well-being will ask me about that. Then I'd know for sure whether or not I'm under surveillance. Well, no one has said a word to me!" she shouted in frustration.

I looked throughout the passageway and finally told her that I could not see any evidence of surveillance equipment.

Dominique continued in a very serious tone. "You know, sometimes the high life has very harmful and disastrous consequences in people's lives. It can kill and destroy them. The fancy and hip magazines tell people that sin is gray. Well, its black-widow black. You heard of the black widow spider?" she asked me.

"Yes, I have," I answered.

"Guess which sex bites the worst?" she asked, but wanted no reply. "It's the female, and then she eats her mate. Do you honestly see many women sticking up for each other? No, they bite you swift and deadly. Women's liberals try to control the actions of other women through trickery. They're not trying to free us from oppression. They are trying to see that we stay oppressed. If your situation is useful to them you might get some help; but, if it isn't, forget any support. If a woman is in trouble, it isn't unusual to hear other women laughing and blaming her, even if she's in the right. The justice system listened to my husband's lying lawyers, and guess which one of us is now homeless? A lot of judges take the side of the males because that's the side where there's money and power. It doesn't matter about the overwhelming evidence against them. I know. The high life made my husband greedy, too. He was successful and supposedly a humanitarian, but it wasn't enough for him. Then I wasn't good enough. Then the children weren't enough. He did it to all of us. Now, do you understand how I feel about being on the government housing programs?" she asked, defying me to prove her wrong.

Dominique gradually began to fill in details of her life, admitting some of her mistakes along the way. "I came from a family of high social position, but was never really interested in what they wanted for me. I stayed away from things I shouldn't have, and didn't stay away from things I should have. I didn't want all the trappings that came with the lives of the rich and famous. Their highs were never high enough or fast enough, and they always had to be buying something, going somewhere, doing something, or doing something to somebody else. These people can't entertain themselves. I believe they are spoiled and lack good values. That's their problem. They resemble machines but expect others to maintain, entertain, and work for them. Well, I entertained all right, until I dropped. And I was the one who felt terrible. Can you beat that? More dead flowers piled high on the earth. The dead never really leave, you know," Dominique said sorrowfully, once again talking in riddles I couldn't quite solve.

Dominique changed the subject, saying, "I believe I had a heart attack from all the stress,… something bad happened to me. I can't remember exactly what it was, though. I haven't seen my children for a long time, but my time will come. In the past, my friends and family have tried to connect me with people who will hurt me and put an end to my desires, but I won't let them. No! No! No! I don't want that to happen to me again!" Her abrupt exclamations were somewhat disconcerting, but then she calmed herself just as abruptly. "I don't want to think about or talk about my parents and family. Everyone was so reckless with my heart. No wonder things went wrong with it!"

Although she was obviously articulate and intelligent, and even had a home of sorts, this woman still felt the strains of living on the street, and her attention could wander without warning. "My skirt is soiled, so I must go to a place where it can be cleaned. I'm thankful for the good things I've been able to keep … for my long walks, especially. It's time to begin my walk once again," she informed me.

Dominique remained seated and sat quietly for a few moments before giving me these parting words, "Many daughters and wives are desired, asked for, given, used and abused, put in harm's way, rejected, then told to go away and are forgotten. 'Mother' is my most important name. I don't forget. I would love for someone to call me 'Mother' again. Many people ridicule and despise me for my lifestyle as I walk the neutral ground, but it's my way." Having said that, she tucked and secured her belongings on the cart and slowly wheeled it out of the alley, setting out once again on her rounds.

I watched her push her cart up the street, still in awe of the way she held herself. Her demeanor conveyed to others that she had indeed lived in a "big house on the hill." Dominique obviously still had a great deal of dignity and pride. The quality of her education and upbringing were unmistakable, but her statements were vague and fragmented and left me wondering. I believe that some of the paths she's been down were terrifying. I can only imagine what a fascinating woman she was before her life turned so tragic, as she remained magnetic even in her reduced circumstances.

* * *

I decided to contact a nearby church to see if they would make sure her medical condition was monitored from time to time. I didn't really understand what happened to her in her lifetime, but I believe several tragedies have hurt her deeply, causing some paranoid behavior, shown by her fear that other people are spying on her and plotting to destroy her and take away her freedom. Dominique has had a lot of time to think about her life, but I don't believe she has really focussed on more than a few of the events that happened or on what went wrong.

One can never fully know or understand the past or predict the future of our "sisters of the road." Where did she go on the long walks she spoke about? Had those hands played a musical instrument? done housework? designed or created fashion clothing or art work? carried a satchel for her ballet attire? combed a child's hair? I was confounded by the wide range of mysteries Dominique had unfolded about her life, but I hadn't learned enough to solve them.

I had taken many notes in shorthand as she spoke, and I immediately jotted down other things I could remember of our conversation after she left. Of all the conversations recorded in this book, this one is more a paraphrase than a transcription. Yet Dominique was so striking and her conversation so impressive that I feel confident in this presentation of the events recorded here.

Two years after meeting Dominique, the bayou country called me back to where I'd first met her. I tried to find her, but her home in the passageway had been remodeled for new businesses and she had had

to vacate her quarters some time before. Even though she was a homeless woman with a "home" and no real desire to change, this uproot-
ing must have hurt her and showed that she was as vulnerable to this
as well as the constant dangers of the open street as were other homeless women who were not so at ease with the situation.

As I searched, she was always one step ahead of me. I learned from
a merchant that Dominique was living under a bridge on the river. I
searched for her along the banks, but her possessions were not to be
found, nor was she. I contacted several business owners and social
and religious organizations about Dominique's whereabouts. She
hadn't been seen for a few weeks, and no one seemed to know exactly
where she was living. One local merchant told me that Dominique is
supposed to take medication for her mental problems, and, when she
doesn't, she can cause a lot of chaos in their shops. That may well have
been the behavior I witnessed when I first met her at the coffee house.
The owners of an art shop told me that she frequents their place quite
regularly and is an expert in some art categories.

I also learned from reliable sources that she was a member of a
prominent family from the east coast. After her marriage, she settled
in this beautiful city with her husband, a physician. He badly mistreated her, being both physically and mentally abusive, if not crimi-
nal. They had a young daughter and possibly a son also, as she did
refer to her "children." She became ill, in part, no doubt, because of
the extreme stress in her marriage. Subsequently, her husband divorced
her and moved back to the east coast. It was her decision to stay in
New Orleans and raise her children. She had legal custody of her daughter, but her husband had visitation rights. In compliance with those
rights, Dominique made arrangements to fly her daughter to him for
a visit. The airplane crashed and the little girl died in the tragic accident. The pictures she wore on her necklaces and displays on the cart
were of her little girl. To this day, so I was told, Dominique frequently
walks to the airport and waits for the airplane that will bring her daughter back home to her. She says she will never leave this city with its
architectural splendors, voodoo secrets, and dried flowers, nor will
she give up her "walks." Her loved ones are coming back home and she
must meet them.

Will Dominique ever return to society, or has she been so physically and emotionally damaged by the events in her life that she sim-

ply cannot find her way back? These are questions that as yet have no answer. Her case is difficult. I hope that she will some day consent to receive help and counseling from those who sincerely want her to recover. As Eleanor Roosevelt said, "I would like … to see us take hold of ourselves, look at ourselves, and cease being afraid." Dominique is dealing with her tragedies in her own private way. She has chosen her current lifestyle, and, for the present time, wishes to keep it.

Cheryl ===

I MET CHERYL at a women's emergency shelter in southern Virginia. Upon arriving at the shelter, I first met Viola, the executive director of the facility, and explained to her my desire to interview a homeless woman staying there. Almost immediately, Viola told me that she had the perfect woman for me—a real survivor with a success story. Viola said that Cheryl had been a homeless woman at the shelter and had worked her way up to the position of house manager. I was asked to wait in the lobby for Cheryl to return, because it was the day of the week she drove a van around town gathering food, clothing, furniture, and other supplies donated by local citizens. Each time the front door opened I looked up, hoping to see Cheryl entering the shelter. I wasn't the only one anxiously awaiting her return. Several of the homeless women staying there had gathered and were waiting to help her unload supplies. All of a sudden Cheryl burst through the front door, creating a whirlwind of activity. She instructed several women where they were to put the precious cargo. Cheryl seemed friendly and outgoing to everyone, but she was definitely in charge. One of the women was so excited about the items that you'd have thought she'd just won the lottery; instead, however, she had several pounds of butter, and she told me they were "like gold" to her.

When the women at the shelter had been assigned their tasks, Cheryl went to speak to Viola. After a few minutes, Cheryl returned and introduced herself, adding, "I understand you'd like to interview me about my homelessness and how I worked my way out of it. I'm a proud person today, but if this shelter hadn't opened its door to me in my darkest hour, I don't know where I'd be now."

Cheryl was striking—tall, pretty, and self-assured. She wore jeans and a blue-and-white-striped oversized blouse. Her dark hair was pulled back into a bun, with thin strips of leather woven throughout it—very creative and attractive, I thought. She wore small, gold loop earrings. Her only visible makeup was a salmon or coral lip gloss, which highlighted her perfectly shaped white teeth when she smiled. Her shimmering light brown skin was flawless, having an almost iridescent quality to it. Cheryl's personality was of the outgoing, matter-offact but friendly, take-charge variety, and she exuded a lot of energy.

After directing me to follow her to a laundry room in the basement, Cheryl explained that she had to put away supplies and load the washers with linens and bedding while we talked or there wouldn't be any clean beds at the shelter that night. "I'm running late today so I'll have to tell you my story as quickly as I can. We must be ready for the women coming into the shelter this evening." She pulled up a chair next to a table used for folding laundry for me to sit on.

Cheryl began loading the washers while telling me her story. "I drove a metro bus in Washington, D.C., for ten years before I drove myself to the streets. I was making a lot of money, more than $40,000 a year, and had $50,000 in my savings account. A nice little nest egg for a young chick. Very good money for someone who didn't go to college, or want to. I wasn't traveling alone in life. I'd met my guy, Harold, somewhere down the line, and he had every quality I'd ever wanted in a man. He was stable, dependable, made more money than I did, loved me, and was a decent human being. He's a prince of a man, and I'm lucky he's still with me after what I put him through," she began.

"I guess I've wondered more than once what went wrong in my life, and I've decided that I probably just got bored. Girl, can you imagine? Looking back, I hadn't known when I was well off! I was living a very carefree life—didn't have any bills to pay and no kids to raise. Not much to worry about. I suppose I had too much money, too much free time, and no real interests or goals."

It was apparent that I would not need to ask many—if any—leading questions. Cheryl was as ordered in telling her story as she was in performing her duties at the shelter. She continued, "My mother died when I was five years old, so I never really knew her. My father sent me to upstate New York for his sister to raise after my mother's death. My auntie raised me with her four kids and sent every one of them to college. She wanted to send me too, but I just didn't want to go. It was that simple. She tried her best to talk me into going, but I couldn't be persuaded. The burning fire to enroll just wasn't there. She did teach me, though, that there is nothing in this world you can't do if you set your mind to do it.…

"Anyway, after I was on my own, I started experimenting with drugs. That was my first step on the road to disaster and homelessness. I have no one to blame for my drug problem except myself. I started smoking marijuana, moved on to snorting cocaine. Smoking crack came next, and finally the big horse—heroin. My body systems were going wild! Looking back, I wonder what I was trying to do—get higher and higher until I really reached heaven? It is easy to overdose. My addiction became so intense that I was doing drugs before I went to work, and even while I was driving a bus through the streets of our nation's capital. The bus-driving scene in the movie *Speed* probably didn't hold a candle to riding with me. Up one street and down another I went, driving wildly all the way. I was always looking for an opportunity to stop the bus for another fix. Some days my routes seemed to go on and on for way too long. I'd get really crazy. On one of my worst days, out of desperation, I unloaded all my passengers and snorted my stuff. I can't remember where I unloaded them. All I know is that when I started coming down from my high all my passengers were gone. I only hoped that I hadn't driven up too many wrong streets, one-way streets, areas not on my route, missed stops, insulted anyone, or worse. I hate to think of all the things I might have done that day while under the influence. Saying I was 'out of control' is definitely an understatement.

"One morning I woke up so ill and in need of a fix that I went to my drug dealer before going to work, just so I could start my day. I bought more drugs to take with me on the bus. Nearly every time the bus was empty of passengers I snorted the stuff. I was so high I almost had an accident. I prayed, 'Lord, if you'll let me get this bus back to the garage safely I'll never do drugs again.'" Although she got the bus back safely, she soon forgot her vow, telling her supervisor that she wanted to take sick leave. "I never went back. The choice was mine. It was either my job or the drugs, and at that time in my life I chose the drugs.

"Drugs were my life for the next three years. It took Harold two years before he knew I was using them. Drug addicts can hide the fact they're users if they want to. They usually become the best liars in the world, something they can really be proud of. Addiction is their dirty little secret, and they can hide it from most people who aren't educated in the world of drugs. I went through all my savings and a lot of Harold's savings without his permission. Finally, after all our savings were gone, I took his bank card and withdrew $275 each morning, leaving enough in his account so he always had lunch money. Harold had a habit, too—eating. At noon I'd sneak out of the house and withdraw another $225 to sustain my $500 a day habit. This was my routine for almost a month until Harold realized he was missing money from his account. After he tightened the reins on his bank account, I started cashing his payroll checks. I was totally out of control! Harold could have sent me to jail, but thank the Lord he loved me and didn't prosecute. He kept a closer watch on his money after he discovered my withdrawals. I was making withdrawals, and I was having them.... It was a full-time job."

I had no time to ask questions. Cheryl rapidly went on with her story—just telling the essential facts without any real embellishment. But there was a sense of unreality in seeing the accomplished busy woman in front of me while hearing of what seemed to be a hopeless case of personal loss and dependence. She reached the point where her drug troubles threatened her home and relationship.

"My man Harold said, 'You're going to enroll in a drug rehabilitation program, or I'm going to leave you!' He knew I would have to be forced into a program, because I had an attitude and wouldn't get clean on my own. I never stayed in any program long enough to have much success. After the first thaw, I thought I could lick the habit anytime I wanted to—remember, I had an attitude. You know, I wasn't going to do this and I wasn't going to do that. I wasn't a drug addict. I just used occasionally. I was still in a state of denial. Finally, Harold said, 'If you don't finish this program, I'm for sure going to leave you.' Right then and there I knew he wasn't leaving, but I had to act like I was going to carry out his wishes. The longest time I'd ever stayed in a program was five days. I'd just leave at my first opportunity. This time, however, I miraculously stayed with the treatment until I was clean. When I was released, I stayed home and took care of the house. I felt good. I became pregnant. I had struggled to fight the temptation to stay off drugs and had won.

"I felt so proud when my first child was born. I knew now that I could get through a program and leave the drugs alone, and the best part was that I'd done what I'd needed to do to have a healthy baby. Two days after the baby's birth I was back on drugs. I challenged myself, you know. I just *knew* I could quit using drugs any time I decided to. All I had to do was return to a treatment center. I knew this. I started staying out at night doing this and doing that, so my man, once again, got fed up with me," Cheryl declared, her expression becoming more serious.

I had no time to express my shock or question her about her relapse, especially since she had expressed such pride in her accomplishment of coming clean. She was already moving along with her story. "Harold learned that his mother was sick down in southern Virginia, so he said, 'I'm going to leave this town behind me and go take care of my mother. I'm also going to take the baby.' 'No! You're not taking my child!' I screamed. Harold insisted, 'Cheryl, you've got to get away from your friends who do drugs and from the other bad influences around this town. Come with me if you want to be a family.'"

Cheryl continued, "I didn't want to go but thought it probably was best. We moved in with his mother and it wasn't long before she found out that I was on drugs. She didn't want anything more to do with me, and said, 'You're a no good bitch. Stay away from me!' Every day she kept dogging me and dogging me. I just got sick and tired of her negative criticisms and interference in my life. I felt down and nervous because I couldn't have drugs. Her attacks on me were nonstop and just pushed me further down into a state of worthlessness. That's what she was doing to me the whole time I was living in her home, so I decided to find a job. When my first paycheck came, I left town.

"Excuse me, I still have poor thoughts about what that woman did to me," Cheryl said, as she grimaced and stopped what she was doing to put her hands to her eyes. After a few moments, Cheryl resumed her story. "I left my son with his father and grandmother and returned to Washington, D.C., to do more drugs. I was stoned again, back in the city of monuments. I stayed a few months and got tired of the drug scene, and also missed my family, so I returned to southern Virginia. I told Harold that I was ready to settle down this time. With Harold being in love with me like he was, he said, 'okay.'

"We rented a small apartment and Harold moved out of his mother's nice big home. He was working and I got a job too. Nine months later we had another child. During my pregnancy I struggled, but again I managed to stay off drugs and had another healthy baby. Then one day I just stopped working and started using drugs again. Same old routine. My man Harold once again said, 'This is it! I can't take any more.' At morning's first light I dressed my oldest child and acted like I was going to the store. I told Harold that I needed some money for groceries and took all the money he had in his wallet. My child and I left immediately for the District of Columbia. I wanted to do crack down by the Potomac with my friends. I thought for sure that stealing all Harold's cash and deserting him would be the end of our relationship.

"My man Harold took me to court, and when I arrived totally intoxicated, I sabotaged any chance I had of getting custody of my kids. The female judge looked at me like I was crazy, and I returned the look. I figured right away that it was over for me, so I started talking trash to her, saying, 'Your honor, you know what? I don't care about the kids … he can have them.' I immediately had to return my oldest child to Harold in Virginia. All the while, I was so hurt.

"After the trial was over, I went back to the district. All I did was cry when I got back there. I asked my brother who lived in the suburbs if he would help me. He said, 'Sure, I'll help you all I can.' Well, he found out that I was using drugs and said, 'Get out!' He put me out of his house and into the cold snow.

"I was wet, freezing and dirty. I couldn't remember my last meal. Come to think of it, I couldn't remember much of anything of late. I began thinking out loud, creating a script from my thoughts: 'Avoid the drug dealers. No, I can't live without my drugs. I have no money, so a dealer won't give me any drugs. Don't make a drug dealer mad or you'll be gotten rid of—they're meaner than a hundred-pound weasel! Okay, find some friends.' Suddenly, the loud engine noise of a city bus snapped me out of my trance and I remembered that I'd once driven one. I had money back then and a nice apartment. I respected myself. Other people respected me too. Deep in my spirit I knew that I was better than this. I'd done my best, or worst, to destroy my life. Now, even my brother didn't care what happened to me. I had exhausted all efforts to come up with a plan as to where to turn for help. Still sitting on the steps in front of my brother's place, I screamed, 'What am I going to do?!'"

I was listening; Cheryl definitely didn't need my help or prodding to help her tell her story! She went on, mechanically doing her washing tasks as she slipped ever more completely back to those bleak days of her life.

"I sat motionlessly, looking up into the falling snow," Cheryl continued. "I needed a hand to help me stand up, but decided to get up myself, since there was no one else around to pick me up anymore. I walked to a friend's apartment. She wasn't home, so I walked about a mile to another friend's apartment. I was freezing but didn't feel much—like a zombie in a trance. I knew I really had only one option. I would have to ask my friend if she would let me make a long-distance phone call to Harold. It was the right thing to do, but would he want me back after what I'd done to him and the kids? I would just have to convince him that I would elevate myself to their level and deny myself drugs forever. I knew it would be worth all my pain and suffering. I prayed my friend would let me use her telephone to make the call. I didn't have many friends left now that I was broke and couldn't bring drugs with me on my visits. I was tired of being a burden to others and carrying around a feeling of worthlessness. I said to myself, 'Cheryl, focus, focus—you've got to focus and pull yourself out of this drug nosedive or your gonna die!' I could feel it happening.

"I followed my heart and called Harold in Virginia, pleading, 'Honey, I know I've lied to you in the past. I know I've done this and I've done that.' He said, 'Well, let's talk about it.' He's quite a guy. Unbelievable. I told him that if he would give me another chance I'd change for good. I'd stop using drugs before coming back to Virginia. I'd find a homeless shelter in the town where he lived and would work there until I could find a job. I'd save my money so I could get an apartment on my own. When I'd been drug free for a year, and had done all the things I'd promised, I'd give him a call. He said, 'Well, that's what you're going to have to do to live with me and the children.'

"I stayed in D.C. for three months before returning to Virginia, knowing that I had to be drug free before any shelter would accept me. I needed the time to dry out. I was ready. This time I was really serious. I knew it was my last chance and I'd have to be stronger than I'd ever been in my whole life. For those three months I lived in a hell only addicts know. Demons danced in my head while my body waged the battle to withdraw and survive.

"When I got to Virginia, I called a women's shelter. 'There are no openings here,' a woman answering my call told me. I panicked but kept my wits until I found a number listed as a 'Women's Emergency

Shelter.' I only had twenty cents in my purse and needed another nickel to make the call. I asked a man on the street if he had a nickel I could have to make the call. The man asked, 'What's in it for me?'

"I didn't have the energy to beg," Cheryl said. "I just looked at him and said, 'Please.' A miracle happened when an angel answered the telephone at the Women's Emergency Shelter and told me to come immediately. When the door at the shelter opened, the director hugged me tightly and invited me in," Cheryl reported.

The director was Viola, who immediately reassured the exhausted woman of her welcome. Cheryl was grateful. "It was the moment when I needed her most. She was taking me into a safe place where I could rebuild my life. I was desperate, and extremely grateful. We stepped inside and she gave me encouragement. After the shelter program and rules were discussed, we began to fill out my application for residency. A calm feeling came over me as I looked around. I wondered how I could ever be able to rejoin society again as a normal contributing person. I glanced around the room and noticed a plaque hanging on the wall, and read the comforting words."

I copied the words of this plaque that had helped assure and inspire cheryl, hoping they way serve a like function with others who may read this book:

> Promise yourself to be so strong that nothing can disturb your peace of mind. To talk health, happiness and prosperity to every person you meet. To make all your friends feel that there is something in them. To look at the sunny side of everything and make your optimism come true. To think only of the best and expect only the best. To be just as enthusiastic about success of others as you are about your own. To forget the mistakes of the past and press onto the greater achievements of the future. To wear a countenance at all times and give every living creature you meet a smile. To give so much time to the improvement of yourself that you have no time to criticize others. To be too large for worry, too noble for anger, too strong for fear and too happy to permit the presence of trouble.
> —Christian D. Larson

Cheryl's story proceeded to the present. "I've worked hard at this shelter and have made good use of the money I've earned. I've kept my savings account papers from my first paycheck forward to the present. I remember when I finally had enough money for a deposit on an apartment and could leave the shelter. It was a day of great celebration for me. I found a nice little place I could afford and lived there for a year, but continued working here at the shelter. After keeping the last of my promises to Harold, I called him on the phone and he came to me. What a joyous reunion," Cheryl said proudly, but with misty eyes. "Harold told me, 'You've proven yourself, girl. Let's get back together for good this time!'

"It was touch-and-go for a while because Harold was nervous, and who could blame him after what he'd been through. I stayed home with the kids and didn't work for about nine months after we got back together. Many a morning as I bathed the kids, I just stared at them and touched their happy little faces. I was so thankful for this miracle. Over and over I told them, 'You are such a blessing. You are such a blessing,'" Cheryl related, genuinely grateful for her life that was now shared with her family.

Cheryl explained her return to the work force. "One day I got a call from Viola, my angel lady from this shelter. She is my heart, a really treasured friend. If it wasn't for her, I wouldn't be where I am today. Viola knew me as a resident and I could talk to her. As a matter of fact, the day I was leaving she told me, 'Cheryl, if you ever need a job, please come back and see me because I like your work ethic and I like you.' I love this lady. She offered me a position as shift coordinator. I worked at that job for about two years and then advanced to house manager.

"I've learned that a person just has to make up their own mind whether or not they want to succeed in life, and when they do, staying focused until their dream is achieved is the answer. My brother always told me, 'Cheryl, solve your problems so you won't go on being a drug addict. No one in our family is a drug addict and I know you're not a career druggie.' I hadn't really listened to anyone when I was heavily into drugs, but after my brother told me that, I thought to myself, 'Girl, you don't look good anymore; drugs are destroying you slowly but surely. You are going to lose your looks and your brains. Maybe you've already lost them and just don't realize they're gone. Maybe your health will fail you before you get a hold of your habit. Look at yourself, only 110 pounds on a 5'-11" frame. You're a walking skeleton! You wear a size six dress, the same size you wore in the fifth grade. Those figures don't add up to a normal healthy proportioned woman. What will become of you and your kids?' What still amazes me is that I was able to stay focused and become a house manager," Cheryl said, gratified by her progress and the feeling that she'd come full circle.

"I express my thoughts aloud quite often around here, saying, 'Thank you, Lord, for the strength you've given me to get where I am today. It's nothing short of a miracle.' My life was a calamity during my drug years, and I recall when no one could tell me anything. I wasn't going to listen to reason. If a person told me that I looked bad, I'd say, 'Bad, what are you talkin' about?' And, every once in a while, I remember the reality check I got when the snow and cold air hit me in the face after landing on that snowy sidewalk in front of my brother's place—alone, with no money and nowhere to go. When my money had run out, so did my so-called friends. I remember one day when I went to a girlfriend's apartment with close to $500 worth of crack cocaine. When the party for two was over, my good friend said, 'Cheryl, I'm having company early tomorrow morning, so you can't stay here any longer.' It was three o'clock in the morning and the rain was pouring down outside. I thought she was kidding until she got ignorant with me. 'Just let me get a few hours sleep,' I begged her. 'No,' she said, and she forced me to leave her warm apartment and walk out into the night. I was so stoned it was unbelievable, and, my Lord, I was so tired. Once again, I had no place to go and I was broke. The end of the line, literally...."

As Cheryl began to share scattered details of her actual homeless period and the years she was involved with drugs, her accomplishment in surmounting them seemed even more impressive and her pride in her accomplishment more understandable. Although I believe that women can rise above their homeless condition, whatever its accompanying reasons, it would not be right to pretend or say that this would be easy. It would be extremely difficult for almost any of us—and then think how much more so for a person whose brain or will might be weakened by drugs or whose heart or spirit is broken by the personal tragedy that led to the homeless situation. In most cases, it is only through the love, strength, caring, and opportunity provided by a person like Viola that even strong women like Cheryl can rise above their homeless situation.

Cheryl continued: "Over the years I'd thought that being a good

talker had really paid off for me. I had always taken my strong personality and good talkin' mouth to my meetings with drug dealers. I talked
my way out of trouble time and time again. Never did I sell my body
for the drugs I needed. I've talked all night long to avoid that particular situation. I thought highly of my body, and always have, and yet
abused it with drugs. I could feel, though, that my good and bad days
and ups and downs were draining my spirit and my health. Every day
was beginning to be a struggle. Soon, I couldn't tell the good ones
from the bad. Those memories are not pleasant." Cheryl told of her
shame thinking of those days, and the fear she now feels for what she
should have felt then. "I try to look at the best parts of my life now and
that is where the pride shows up. I've been with the same wonderful
man for ten years and we have two great kids. He would marry me
today if I would just say yes. I've always believed that things change for
a couple after they marry, and not always for the best. I say, 'it's only a
piece of paper,' but I know that some pieces of paper are very important and valuable in this life. I'm afraid of that marriage license paper,
though. My Harold was married once before and has two teenaged
kids. I figure he's already been married and it hadn't worked out for
him, so maybe marriage wouldn't work for us either. Right, wrong, or
otherwise, that's the way I think, but I know he loves me. Sometimes
I'm uncertain about my role, though, and how it should be played.
You know, the legal rights I have, or won't have, when I get older and
need a pension and so forth," Cheryl said, expressing her concerns
about not being legally married.

I was able to learn a bit more about the earlier days of Cheryl's
troubles, hoping to better understand how the destructive cycle began. In Cheryl's case, as in countless others, there seems to have been
no defining moment, just a bit of rebelliousness here, some experi-
mentation there, and then an increasing series of bad choices in friends,
actions, or attitudes.

"Remembering back to the beginning of my 'lost' period, as I call
it, my aunt was deeply hurt and disappointed when she learned that I
was on drugs. I didn't hide anything from her. When she asked me if
what she'd heard was true, I said, 'Yes, I'm on drugs. I don't know
when I'm coming off them either, but I'll let you know when I do.'
Obviously, I had a little attitude with her. I didn't have to say all that I
said. This woman did everything in the world for me and treated me
like her own daughter. I felt terrible that I had let her down. It was no

way to talk to, or treat, someone who had raised me and had shown so much love for me. Her great spirit and hopes for me meant nothing when drugs came into my life. I told her I wasn't going to do anything stupid or get myself killed (as if I'd have anything to say about it). I still remember her saying, 'I hope you know what you're doing.' I know she worried a lot and lost a lot of sleep over me, but we're fine now. I call my wonderful aunt every now and then to see how she's doing. I caused her great pain, and for that I feel ashamed. It felt so good during the last Christmas season to be able to send her money. She moved from New York to South Carolina a while back. Her health is good and she says she's fine.

"I'd thought my daddy hadn't loved me when he sent me to auntie's home, but of course I was too young to understand. Before he died, I thanked him for what he'd done for me and for sending me to his sister's home. I told him I was grateful for the upbringing and love I'd experienced in my life. I did have a lot of love around me.

"I had a rendezvous with drugs and flirted with disaster, but escaped in time to live a fulfilling life. Some of my friends weren't so lucky. Many of them are dead. I'm so proud of myself now. I've come so far. I don't hide my story from the ladies staying here at the shelter, either. They come in and try to con me, like I don't know what's going on! They say, 'You don't know what it's like to be homeless.' I say, 'Well, excuse me! Yes, I do. Don't tell me that I don't know how it feels to be homeless. I do. I used to stay in this same shelter, in that room, slept in that same bed, and worked very hard when I first came here.' If just one woman is saved from a life of drugs and homelessness, I will feel good about telling my story. I want to tell them flat out—my downfall started when I accepted that first joint of marijuana. I believe the education against drugs must start in the home and at school as soon as a child is old enough to understand what's being said.

"It's so nice to have the burden of homelessness lifted from my life. I've always wanted a home of my own and now my dream has been realized. I've said a thousand times, 'Lord, if you'll let me live to see another day, I'll never do drugs again!' I'd recover and then relapse and have to start all over. I don't want to think about the hurt I've caused my loved ones or the damage I've done to my body. Oh, and I especially don't want to think about all the money I've wasted. I've apologized many times to those I've hurt and it only brings me pain to recall my past mistakes." With those words, disclosures, acknowledgments, and vows, Cheryl concluded the story of her homelessness and her fight against drugs.

Cheryl resumed her duties at the shelter after our interview; but, before I left, she added, "I'm happy with where I am today … right here at this shelter with other women who need help and guidance. I hope to repay my debt for the help I've received here. Now if someone asks me if I've left a posterity or a mess, a posterity will be my answer."

Saige ===============================

AT A SHELTER in Las Vegas, Nevada, called the Shade Tree I saw a lady with a little boy one afternoon as they arrived there. As I looked at the woman more closely I saw a terrible sight. She was exhausted almost to a point of total collapse and was nervous and trembling as she pulled the young boy close to her side. The skin of both was covered by what appeared to be scabies—a red rash causing them to constantly scratch themselves, further inflaming their skin. The woman's face was flushed, either from the hot temperature outside or from high blood pressure. I believed she needed hospitalization.

I watched them make their way to the front desk and, while waiting to be helped, the woman read signs on the wall proclaiming the worth of each person and that each life has "great purpose." Another said, "Reach for Your Dreams." It was not apparent that she believed the messages. The woman told the director that she and her grandson had just traveled more than a thousand miles in 100° heat. She said that she was homeless, looking for work, and very ill, and that her grandson was also ill. The woman paused for a few moments before continuing, "I haven't been able to buy the medications I've needed for over a year, and without them my high blood pressure, thyroid condition, hormone deficiency, allergies, and skin condition have worsened considerably."

The director was a caring and extremely efficient woman; just being in the same room with her made me feel like I had a mother again. She called the University Medical Center (UMC) for medical help for the itinerant pair. However, it was necessary for them to travel to the UMC by bus. The shelter provided the tokens, but I wondered if the woman and child were too ill for the trip. I volunteered to help them get on the bus and stay at the UMC while they were being treated.

We made a brief acquaintance then, but their condition made me feel that it would be inappropriate to develop a conversation at that time. When we arrived at the hospital, the little boy was immediately taken to a room where he was bathed and given an injection and medication for his skin condition and open sores. Knowing her grandson was getting care calmed the grandmother considerably. After a brief physical examination, it was discovered that the woman's blood pressure was critically high—such that a stroke could occur at any time. The staff worked diligently to aid her. The woman looked defeated as she told the technician, "I'm so exhausted from my life right now that I can no longer think clearly or remember things like I should. I can't concentrate or focus on important things, and I may even be a safety hazard to myself and others while driving my car."

After the woman was cared for, she told the attendant that she felt much better and wanted to return to the shelter with her grandson. "I don't have any money or insurance, and I'll be fine at the shelter after I get some rest," she maintained. She looked over at me and said, "Boy, I've caused some commotion here tonight, haven't I?" "We all need help sometime in our lives," I replied. She then matter-of-factly described her situation: "I'm fifty-five years old with a grandchild to raise, and I'm homeless. God help me. I've run life's gamut—been both rich and poor. I've married and divorced twice, even though one marriage was enough. I have five living children and several grandchildren. I've traveled and lived in places around the world, had beautiful homes, had talent, had looks, had social position, had high-paying jobs, and now I'm homeless. I'm really a farm girl at heart, but was uprooted from the farm life I loved and have been transplanted several times during my life," she said, in a relieved and more talkative state after her medical treatment, especially after she became aware of my interest in her situation.

The three of us boarded a bus for our return to the Shade Tree. While the staff was preparing a room for the homeless woman and her grandson to sleep in, we talked. She introduced herself—I will call her Saige—and told me that her six-year-old grandson's name was Will and that he'd been born with a neurological disorder and needed constant supervision, as he could become very unruly or easily get into trouble. I introduced myself and told Saige that I was at the shelter to interview homeless women. After a few moments, she replied, "I'd like to tell you about how I became homeless, but I can't tonight because I'm too tired to talk anymore." We agreed to talk in a few days. I was very pleased that she wanted to give me an interview, and I looked forward to hearing her story.

After a few days had passed, I returned to interview Saige at the Shade Tree. She was waiting for me in the lobby area when I arrived, and Will was playing with toys and being supervised by an attendant. They both appeared to be feeling more comfortable. Saige informed me, "I seem to be confused about the years and events. I tend to ramble, but I'll do my best to tell other women about how this dog jumped through hoops for twenty-six years and where it got her."

I felt certain that Saige wasn't a dog by any stretch of the imagination. Her strawberry-blond hair fell below her shoulders and was gathered at the nape of her neck by a navy blue and white scarf. Her features were beautiful—sparkling blue eyes and a fantastic smile. She was maybe 5 feet 4 inches in height and her figure was almost athletic, yet feminine. She was dressed in a shirt and jeans. I began to notice that she still scratched her skin occasionally, except for her face, which was probably the only place where she didn't have the rash.

Saige began her story. "I had the same dreams as most girls growing up in the 1950s and 1960s. We were all striving to earn our high school diplomas, get a good job after graduation so we could buy all the things our parents couldn't afford, and, of course, marry Prince Charming. I was on my way! I had my diploma, a good job, and was ready for the white picket fence. I dated several boys during my high school years, but the boy who has turned out to be the love of my life died in a tragic car accident after an out-of-town football game. I was totally devastated by his death. We were so much alike and were truly soul mates, I've since discovered. When the news of the accident came to me, I cried until I couldn't cry any more. Then I moped around for a couple of years."

Her tale continued. "Finally, I felt a measure of happiness again when Will moved to our town in Wyoming. We seemed to be attracted to each other immediately. A good-looking cowboy with a charming personality seemed to be the combination that stirred my interest. He asked me to go out on double-dates with him and his friends. We went to dances at our high school and church, mostly. We definitely had fun together. My girlfriends were already either married or had announced their weddings in the local newspaper, so I felt like I was getting left behind. Also, I no longer wanted to live at home with my parents. I'd excelled in my high school business courses, so finding a job had been easy for me. I'd even saved enough money to buy some nice furniture for my first home. In those days, not too many girls were going to college; they were 'goin' to the chapel, and were goin' ta get married,' immediately after high school." Wistfully, Saige then remarked, "Somehow, my dreams of living happily ever after with Prince Charming never came true. Even after all these years, I've never forgotten the boy who was killed."

A more skeptical listener certainly might doubt the "true love" of a young girl; but it is certain that she felt the loss of her boyfriend greatly and that it no doubt colored her future expectations and assumed an even greater fairytale quality of bliss as real hardships mounted in her life.

Saige related the details of her first marriage, "I was eighteen years old when Will proposed to me. I remember being nervous the morning of our wedding ceremony, wondering if I was doing the right thing. I was told that it was just wedding jitters and that every bride gets them. I went to our chapel wearing a hand-me-down white wedding dress and held a bouquet of purple violets tied with raffia. Soon afterward, I discovered the stone in my engagement ring was not authentic and should not be confused with even a semiprecious stone, but the silver wedding band seemed to be legit. They were still precious to me.

"We had two children during our marriage, a boy and a girl. Will turned out to be an immature, irresponsible boy, with a bad addiction and some sorry habits. We moved eighteen times during our four years of marriage, usually in the middle of the night. He was always looking for a good game, while my broken heart and tired body were always looking for refuge and a home. There was never money to pay the rent, so the moving continued. I've saved our old love letters in a special box. They were written on the backs of the bad checks he wrote to cover his gambling debts," Saige said, telling her story with wit and enthusiasm.

"Will had the potential for a successful life. He came from a small town in Wyoming, where his father worked the family farm and made an honest living. They were good people. With a little help from his sons, the farm could have grown and prospered, but Will and his brothers didn't have much interest in farming. Will preferred a lifestyle that revolved around bars and gambling. When he did work, his skill was in carpentry. After quitting high school, he worked for a small manufacturing plant; but, unfortunately, in his private life he tore down more than he ever built, and he had a gambling habit that was mangier than a coyote in August. Eventually, he became a burden I just couldn't carry any longer," she revealed.

"Our marriage began to fall apart just three weeks after the ceremony. I was working as a secretary with a successful firm at the time, and one day while at work I got a phone call from a bank teller about some hot checks that had to be picked up. I didn't even know what a 'hot check' was. My father had always handled all our financial affairs with cash. We sold hay and crops; we got money. We sold a beef or pig; we got money. We drove into town and bought what we needed. Simple. I knew the teller had to be wrong because my husband and I didn't have a checking account. Well, it turned out that I was wrong. Will had opened an account, and, yes, I was his legal wife whose name was also on the account. I was absolutely aghast! I made arrangements with the bank to pick up the checks on my payday, which was just a couple of days away. For the next two days I worried myself sick, and I was so ashamed that I didn't confide in anyone. I even thought I might end up going to jail. Why had Will done this to us? This was the beginning of four years of pure hell for me. We seemed to have a deal,... he'd write bad checks to cover his gambling debts, and I'd cover the checks with my wages. A very sweet deal for him. If you're wondering why I let him go on like this, well, now I ask myself that same question. But at such a young age I thought marriage was supposed to be like this ... helping each other. A wife just helped her husband as problems arose."

I listened quietly and was discovering that this woman was very articulate as she told her story, although a certain disjointedness began to confuse me as her tale developed and events from various periods of her life began to be jumbled together. "I found out that Will was living high on the hog. He and his friends were eating at local restaurants, hanging out in places with billiards and pinball machines, and driving his pickup truck up and down Main Street most of the day. I was going hungry, and driving eighty-five miles a day to work my brains out at a desk job. I was packing my own lunch, which consisted of soda crackers and the peaches my mother and I had bottled during the summer. All my money was going to cover his bad checks and pay for our living expenses. My mother told me, 'Saige, you've got to get a food budget, so you'll have enough money to buy your food. You can't continue going to work hungry.'

"No one really knew the sad state my new marriage was in—not even my mother. All she knew was that I never had enough money for food. I was so embarrassed, and for some reason my young mind thought it was my fault and I must deserve what I was or wasn't getting. Why else would Will treat me so badly? I must be a person of little worth and deserve such treatment. I told myself that if I really tried hard I could make things better.

"Will was only working at part-time jobs, so he had lots of time to hold beer parties in our home during the days while I was at work. The guys he bummed around with were losers. When I got home from work each evening, there was usually a big mess for me to clean up from the party thrown that day. Will's buddies were such degenerates, and watched me like a pack of wolves as I cleaned the house. Their eyes followed me and their teeth showed stains from the chewing tobacco they used. Their same old drunken stories and resulting laughter were neverending. You get the picture. Will would invite some of them to spend the night, and sometimes 'the night' stretched into a few days. One morning I caught one of them urinating out our front door. 'What are you doing?' I yelled to the bum who'd just relieved himself.

"He told me with a leer, 'I just opened yer door so I could hear the duet a rooster and a coyote were singin' outside. Ain't it purty?' I gave him the benefit of the doubt and assumed he was referring to the duet. I screamed for Will to kick them all out and told him that no more disgusting types were to be invited to the house. The two of us had no life together," Saige said, still repulsed in her mind remembering the offensive behavior she had tolerated.

Saige looked weary as she relived the events of her trying past. "I finally couldn't cover his bad checks any longer and it caught up with us. One evening five police cars and a couple of disgruntled businessmen were waiting at our house for Will to show up. When Will turned the corner at the foot of the hill, he saw the reception committee that awaited him and immediately backed his pickup truck down the hill and fled to Canada for a while. He worked at different jobs there, just enough to meet his needs. Of course, I didn't receive any help from him while he was gone or any form of communication, but when he finally called I immediately joined him. I guess I thought it was the right thing to do. I'd learned one thing, though, not to cover his hot checks or lie to his bosses about his absences from work."

A pause of a few moments in her story accounted for years of her life. She continued, "Some of the dives Will and I lived in weren't fit for human occupancy. I used to call them 'roach motels.' Each time we moved, the cleaning began all over again. So many rundown shacks had to be cleaned from top to bottom just so we could live in them. We would no more than get settled, usually two to three weeks, when he'd come home and announce, 'Pack up, we're movin' outa here!'

"Will was still working at odd jobs here and there, but he managed to be home long enough to help produce a darling, good-natured, adorable little boy we named Wyatt, after the colorful Mr. Earp, of course. Food was scarce, but I always managed to find enough for Wyatt. Me, I looked like a victim of starvation. I had lost more than twenty pounds since our marriage. When we were near my parents home, they fed me and always gave me money for food. I tried to hide how desperate my situation was, because I knew my parents would worry about us until they were sick. They didn't deserve to suffer from my poor judgment in choosing a partner. Somehow, though, they were onto my plight and were a great support for me. I never told Will about the money they gave me, and saved it to feed Wyatt.

"My family never knew from one day to the next where I'd be living. I'd give them our new address each time we moved, but before they could find us we'd already moved again. Mother said I reminded her of a gypsy woman she once knew back in Illinois. At one point, we lived on a big ranch where Will worked for our room and board. I'll never forget that place. I thought at last Will had found a job where he might better himself. There were no gambling or drinking establishments for more than 300 miles, and the people there were decent and would not lead him astray or tempt him to fall back into his old ways. Well, I was wrong again! We were there maybe six weeks when he announced one evening that we had to 'leave in a hurry.' Years later, I found out that he'd robbed the big freezers at the ranch and taken a huge amount of frozen meat. I still can't figure out how he hid the meat and got it off the ranch without me knowing anything about it. He probably contacted some of his old buddies, and they had met him in an isolated area and helped him by taking and selling the meat. I pictured the whirlwind exchange being made in a ravine somewhere in the back country, with bandanas covering their faces and chaps protecting them from the thorns and scrub oak in the area as they hurriedly transferred the precious, melting cargo in the extremely hot weather."

Saige's reflections had stopped to circle at that point. "I'll never forget that ranch house. It had three bedrooms, a kitchen, a bathroom, and a big L-shaped living room. Apparently, the furnace had blown up when the previous tenants were living there, and they had just moved out. All the walls were sooty. What a mess! I washed and rinsed those walls the entire time we lived there. Every room had to be scrubbed and rescrubbed. I was so worn out and tired from the juggling act of tending my little son, cleaning the house, and trying to raise my husband. The baby was just six months old when we had to 'leave in a hurry' this time. I remember his age precisely because, as I was putting him down in his crib for his last nap in that house, I heard on the radio that Marilyn Monroe, the movie star, was dead. It was August 1962. I also remember thinking, 'if a famous, beautiful, rich woman like Marilyn can't make it in this world, what chance do I have?' I guess she hadn't used any better judgment in her life than I had.

"The moves were actually getting easier. We owned less and less with each move, and our net worth had fallen considerably. The television that I'd paid seven hundred dollars for had been sold for one hundred dollars. Our couch, which had cost me five hundred dollars, also went for one hundred dollars. Nearly all the furniture had been sold for next to nothing. All were sold to pay gambling debts. When I'd leave the house, the furniture seemed to disappear. Will always told me he'd just lent it to friends, but I never saw any of it again. Our clothes and remaining furniture now easily fit in the back of our pickup truck. My wardrobe consisted of my husband's pants and a rope that I used for a belt. I wore his shirts, too. Only one pair of shoes remained in my closet after our yard sales—my cheerleading shoes. Thank the Lord, they were oxfords. My family helped out with baby clothes if they could find us.

"Throughout our marriage, Will stayed away from our home all hours of the day and night. He spent his time drinking, smoking, chewing, and gambling. He still invited his buddies to stay with us until they sobered up or just moved on. They looked and acted so disgusting, and were about as smart as a cow pie. Many nights I walked the floor waiting for him—always worrying and watching every car that passed our house. Divorce from my cowboy-gambler-furniture sales-man husband was not on my program, so I was still comin' out of the chute hoping for more chances at a purse." Sensing my questioning, she explained that "in rodeo talk that means that I wasn't going to give up on my marriage and would hang on until we were financially stable. I'd decided to ride out our troubles. Some nights I'd lock him out of his stable when he came home too late. 'I should have married an old-fashioned girl who'd take it for granted that what I was telling her was the truth, not a modern girl like you who questions everything,' he complained. Yeah, like the Ten Commandments should have been writ-ten on a Web page, I guess. He made me so angry! Damn."

Saige continually interspersed her recitation with expletives—many far stronger than "damn." Although I have chosen not to in-clude them here, I must concede that much of her emotion is lost in the retelling, and I would ask the reader to mentally imagine periodic outbursts and exclamations. She definitely was not just casually recit-ing her tale, although her voice and manner were generally calm, weary, resigned, even matter-of-fact. Early in our interview, in fact, she had apologized for her profanity, confessing that, although she felt it to be wrong, there were times when only a four-letter word was adequate to express her feelings.

She continued, displaying the quick wit that I'd heard quite often in the telling of her story, "At times I visualized the newspaper head-lines: "Teton Tragedy—Saige Kills Husband! Gambling Days Over ... Lead Poisoning Cures Addiction." We were living in the desert high country of Wyoming at that particular time. The call of the wild pin-ball machine was still blowing in his head. How do you tame the wind?" Saige asked rhetorically.

Reflection turned to lament. "If only I'd known what Will was like before I married him. I hadn't known that he was in trouble in his hometown and that for that reason his parents had sent him to be raised by his older brother. I sometimes feel they all played a dirty trick on me by not telling me the true circumstances of Will moving to our town. He basically had a good heart, but that asset never made up for his bad habits. Why hadn't his family told me about his prob-lems and bad habits? It wasn't fair to me. One of Will's habits, even back then, had been gambling. I wish I'd known or been perceptive enough to realize there must have been something wrong or a reason why his parents had sent him to our town. At only eighteen years of age, I wasn't mature enough to figure out what was really going on. You know how teenagers are, though, they think they know everything...."

Her thoughts bounced back and forth through time, somewhat like the pinball image she had linked with her husband. "When I was eight months pregnant with my first child, I thought of suicide. My plan was to freeze to death. I waited until after dark and dressed only in my nightgown. I walked across town to the rodeo grounds in subzero temperature and snow up to my hips. I was going to lie down on the bleachers and just go to sleep. I didn't think anyone would know I was there, because usually there was no activity in the arena on cold winter nights. I would surely freeze to death before being found. My plan was foiled, however, when my sister and her husband came to visit me and just happened to be driving on that side of town and saw me walking. They think it was divine intervention. Who knows? Of course, they picked me up and wrapped me in a blanket and took me home. We talked for hours about my marriage problems and I felt much better. I knew I wasn't alone and there were people who cared about me. I was just crying out for help, because my day-to-day problems were just too much for me to handle. And the problems were all magnified because I was going to bring a child into the world. Will didn't pay attention to me when I'd tell him that I was ill and couldn't take any more of his terrible behavior. I had a dilemma on my hands, and no matter how I handled it, it was wrong. I knew I couldn't stand any more abuse and worry. What were women supposed to do in this situation ... go crazy? Get sick and die? Starve to death? Run away? Commit suicide?

"I'd been so protected in my young life from this type of behavior that I knew absolutely nothing about how to deal with the problems I now faced. I was in a fix, but my early training had taught me to never give up, so I decided to try harder. A separation of any kind wasn't to my liking at this time in my life. I don't ever remember women or teachers of any kind talking to me about divorce. I'd never heard of it. I believe that is why I was stuck in limbo. If Will never shaped up, I didn't know how my life could go on."

As I listened to Saige, I thought about my work and the training of others in crisis intervention and counseling, realizing that here seemed to be a classic case of how a sympathetic ear and counseling could have helped guide a young woman, perhaps helping steer her from the troubles that had led to her homelessness now. Counselors and even friends who listen never know how much heartache their guidance and kindness might help spare other souls. Although some might scoff at what seems a rather melodramatic "suicide" attempt, whether it was real or more pretended, it was a very real cry for help.

"After Wyatt was born, we continued our same old lifestyle, moving from place to place. I just couldn't get enough of the 'good life,'" she remarked bitterly. "Sure, there were still fights after Will came home in the early morning hours, resulting in more tears and absolute heartbreaking misery than I care to remember, but I had Wyatt to enjoy and keep me company, so that helped me cope with the bad parts of my life—kind of leveled out the playing field.

"Less than a year after Wyatt was born, I became pregnant with our second child and wondered how I would ever manage to raise another little one. I'll never forget the night she was born. Will and a buddy were going hunting. They were downstairs cleaning their rifles when my first pain hit. I yelled for Will to come but he didn't hear me, so I crawled downstairs and got his attention. Both he and his buddy were disgusted with me because I was interrupting their hunting plans. Nonetheless, we all left for the hospital in the truck, dropping Wyatt off at Will's aunt and uncle's home on the way. When we got to the hospital, Will slowed down and stopped just long enough for me to get out with my suitcase, unassisted, of course. He said, 'Don't make such a big deal out of giving birth—the Indian women don't. They just squat, have the baby, and get up and go back to work.' Will and his buddy roared off down the street, and I checked myself into the hospital. Maybe I should've checked into 'squatters' rights.' It may have been the only way for me to get a permanent home," Saige said in a sarcastic tone.

Saige's voice trembled as she spoke: "I was finally beginning to see the light. As I carried my suitcase into the hospital alone, I began to cry and my mind mulled over the events that had just transpired.... Will, withdrawing from me, again, never being around when things got tough or when I really needed him. He was never there for Wyatt, either. If it wasn't convenient for him to participate, he didn't. He wasn't worried about my health or that of his newborn child. I continued to volley my doubts and fears back and forth as I filled out hospital admittance papers. Finally, I answered my own question—when things were going swell for him and going his way, he seemed happy, but when they weren't, he didn't seem to want to be around or bothered. He didn't want any responsibility on his shoulders whatsoever. There, I'd focused on the problem. Also, not much thought was going into his immediate or future plans for our family. I could plan until I was blue in the face and it didn't seem to make much difference. I was worried about the big picture, but his big picture seemed only to revolve around his next outing with his friends. I remembered how he laughed at me earlier in the evening and had said, 'You women need to have more fun. You worry too much about keeping the house going. If you do decide to go to a party, you plan about who's going to be there, what you're going to wear, what you're going to bring to eat and on and on. We men ask just two things of a party … that you show up naked and bring beer!' Will always thought everything was a big joke."

Saige said she was still wondering about her future when her labor of childbirth intensified. She decided to focus on the immediate birth of her baby, and figure out what she was going to do with her life when she felt better. She related that she thought simply, "I'm all alone now. Just concentrate and talk yourself through the birth one step at a time and you'll be all right; soon you'll be wheeled into the delivery room."

She continued, "I did what I had to do and soon a small baby girl was born. We hadn't picked out a name for the baby, so I waited for Will to show up—perhaps he had a favorite name for her. I didn't see Will again for two days. I found out that he had been arrested for poaching a deer. I'd saved some money my parents had sent me and hid it in the baby's dresser drawer, figuring Will would never find it there, but he had. He'd told a friend of his to go to the house and get the money and use it for bailing him out of jail. Now I had no money to get my baby girl and me out of the hospital. I called my parents and told them about my predicament. They were several hundred miles away, but they came and paid my hospital bill as soon as they could and took my new daughter and me home. No one will ever know what life was like for me back then.

"After my parents left me and returned to their home, I decided that it was time to take a good honest look at where I stood in my marriage. I pretty much decided that my situation was hopeless. I'd given Will nearly four years to get help for himself and change the direction of his life. Over and over he'd refused to get professional help for his addictions and meant to continue his same course of behavior. He'd made it very clear to me, but I'd chosen not to believe him. He'd broken too many promises and shown too little consideration for both my feelings and those of our little children. He continually betrayed us in one manner or another and showed no concern for our personal welfare. Will displayed no respect for me and had trashed my trust in him. I was the butt of his jokes, yet the mother of his children. To me, this wasn't a combination I found compatible for a good marriage. I decided that I'd been a fool to endure his abuse and didn't want anymore. I also owed a better future to my children. I would let Will know how I felt and would 'shoot from the hip.' It was not to my liking to seek a divorce, because I believed it was a sin; but I also believed that God helps those who help themselves. I intended to help myself and my children from that point on."

Knowing that I hoped to write a book and share her story with others, Saige next spoke to that audience—you, the reader. "Ladies, don't be so naive as to think something like my situation could never happen to you. If a boy isn't a man, or a man doesn't want a commitment or isn't mature enough for a family, you'll definitely receive this kind of treatment, too. Don't kid yourself, and don't 'kid' yourself—I mean get pregnant. Your child deserves better. You deserve better. Your family deserves better. You can't change someone who doesn't want to be changed. Both you and your children will lose, too. So, find a partner who doesn't need to be changed. The same thing goes for a good guy. Don't settle for a woman who has some bad habits or needs a personality overhaul. I remember Will's friends saying, 'We go to restaurants to eat only because we never see a bar fly at the local tavern who wears an apron!' I believe they had something figured out, for a change."

Saige explained how her marriage finally ended. "When my little girl, Cheyenne, was three months old, I called it quits. Hell, I finally came to my senses and decided to stop being such a disgusting doormat. I had reached the end of my rope. The high country moose and I had a lot in common. We both protected our young. My little family had nothing … no home, no steady income, not much food, no furniture, and not much hope. The boy I'd married, who loved the bright lights of the pinball machine and runnin' with the boys, wasn't a person I wanted my children to emulate.

"It was so typical of my time with Will that the last year we were together our Christmas tree was repossessed. An employee from a local store came to our house and produced a bad check that was sup-posed to cover Will's purchases—a Christmas tree, a can of 'chew' for himself, and a few little presents to put under the tree for the children. I couldn't cover the check, so the store employee had me remove my homemade decorations and then repossessed the tree. There was a two-foot hole in the ceiling just above the tree that I'd boarded up so my children wouldn't fall down from the second floor. Suddenly, there was a ripping sound from the ceiling above, just as the tree was losing its ornaments. I looked up just in time to see my son's leg come through the hole. 'I'm okay, momma,' he told me, 'but why are you moving our tree? Is it time to move again?' I told him, 'Yes, but we'll put a tree up at our new house so Santa Claus can find it.' Will had lost our pickup truck in a poker game a few days earlier, so a friend had helped him bring the tree home. I didn't have any idea how we would move our possessions to another place. The only thing I can think of that would have been worse than that Christmas would be knowing there was no Santa Claus, only politicians," Saige said, and laughed loudly. It ap-peared that time had helped heal some of the wounds from the sad times she'd related, although I guess it was just as likely that the bitter-ness of those days left a lingering taste that could only produce a bitter jest. Not really trying to be a reporter and elicit a response to ques-tions, I took my task to be that of a recorder, just listening, and only in the recounting of the event trying to interpret parts of the monologue to assist the understanding of the reader.

Saige's thoughts returned her back in time. "As I look back upon my first marriage, I can truthfully say, 'How sad.' I still believe my hus-band loved me, but his brand of love surely wasn't enough to make us a 'forever' family, and the circle was broken. I know he had a terrible addiction, but he was never physically abusive. We could have had so much fun doing things together, raising our little family, and loving one another. I could have had the white picket fence—he could have built it, too—but it just wasn't in the cards, so to speak."

I was somewhat surprised by her next words—both what they said and how much of a timespan they indicated. "Will was very young when he suddenly died of a massive heart attack. Recently I found the cemetery where he is buried and was able to locate his grave. What a strange feeling it was to wander through the cemetery looking for his marker. The snow was deep, and my thoughts hearkened back to the night I went through my suicide episode. It was a difficult search to find Will's grave. I'm glad the sun was shining. It made my task more bearable. My grandson, who is with me here at the shelter, was with me then also, and he ran from headstone to headstone looking for his grandfather's grave. He will never know the grandfather he was named for. I needed to find his grave so I could close this chapter in my life. I remembered my trip to the rodeo grounds that winter night so many years before, and how I'd wanted to die on a bleacher and be covered by snow. He'd be sorry, I'd thought. Now, he's the one who's buried under the snow, and I'm the one who's sorry. Isn't life full of painful ironies."

Saige continued to muse about her past, then spoke: "Will had the talents to make something of himself, but he just couldn't get a grip on his bad habits. Now, he's buried in the same valley where he grew up. I can clearly recall his little-boy smile, the freckles on his nose, and his curly brown hair. Wyatt is the spitting image of him. As I looked down at Will's headstone, I could hardly believe that the boy I'd loved and married was buried there. I hoped he was at peace.

"While I was in the area, I contacted some of Will's relatives who were still alive. Most of them helped me so much when we'd lived on the ranch. I saw the old weathered barn and the rusted farm equipment that had been parked for good. I'd worked many hours on the tractor just to keep it running. Will's dad had needed help with the mechanics, because his boys were never around to help him—so he taught me the basics. I couldn't help remembering that once it hummed across the fields carrying Wyatt and his grandpa ... just the two of them, laughing and singing. Old Will always wore a big straw hat, with a partial bale missing. Life was so simple then. I remembered the family reunions and outdoor picnics where the older men played horseshoes and children played with water hoses and water balloons, swung from trees into the river, and decorated and rode their bikes in the 4th of July parade. I've never laughed so hard as when the kids rode sheep and calves in the rodeos ... just had a rope on them and hung on for dear life after coming out of the chute. I was overcome with sadness because my children and I had lost this lifestyle, and I wept uncontrollably."

Saige continued, jumping back and forth through years and decades as her story began to take better shape in my mind. "After visiting the old ranch, I went into town to visit with Will's mother, now in her nineties. We talked for several hours about the events that happened in our lives. She was still as sharp as a tack, and she looked me in the eye and said, 'You know, some of Will's wives—there were five—filed for divorces much too soon. They should've given him a longer time to change.' Well, shame on me, I guess! After thinking about it for no longer than a second, I decided that four years had been long enough for me to invest in a seemingly hopeless marriage. Will's father had died a few years back, and to this day I truly miss this wonderful man. All in all, our visit was short and sweet. I visited with two of my sisters-in-law who were very friendly, but the one who was supposed to be the most religious of all refused to see me. I thought that was rich.

"After nearly thirty-three years of soul searching and thinking about my first marriage, I've pretty much decided that I was a hardworking western girl with good morals and simple needs. I did my best to make my marriage work and was honest in all my dealings. I gave it my best shot, but the marriage failed. I've decided to be kind to myself and forgive Will," Saige said in resignation.

Slowly, blanks were filled in as she continued. "At twenty-two, I was snake-bitten again by the first man who asked me for a date after my divorce. I'd thought it was love at first sight and immediately married him. Did I mention I was pregnant? Being so scatterbrained wasn't like me, but the U.S. Army sergeant was very forceful and knew how to exploit my fragile sense of self-worth. I know that now, but I didn't back then. I was young and tried to adapt to his personality. I realize now that he was a predator and I was his prey. My second marriage led to three more children and several miscarriages. When the marriage was over, I swore off marriage forever, and fifteen years later I still haven't accepted a date, although I lusted once or twice. I was so abused by my husbands, both mentally and physically, that I can barely hold the hand or accept a hug from a man. The sad part is they are probably decent and loving men. I decided to give up trying to find a good marriage partner a long time ago, because I can't seem to pick a good man."

Saige explained how she met her second husband, the army sergeant she simply called "Big." "The sergeant was on his best behavior when we first met, and I was too naive to realize that almost everybody starts out this way. He hid the bad side of his personality behind a slick disguise. He'd come from another state, so I knew nothing about his childhood, family, or background. Sound familiar? I should have remembered that I hadn't known anything about Will before marrying him either, and that there was a pattern to my regular way of doing things. But I did not. I hadn't known or realized much about patterns back then—just went with the flow. I wish now that I'd visited his family and found out what he was really like before I got pregnant."

After the wedding, Big soon changed his way of speaking and acting. According to Saige, "He became very loud and bossy. Before long, I suspected he'd probably been the neighborhood bully as a child, because he demanded his own way, insisted on being the center of attention, and became ugly and abusive if things didn't go his way ... or if they did go his way—it really didn't matter. He purposely picked fights and started arguments so he could storm out of the house and come back when he chose to. I didn't figure it out that I'd been purposely set up." Showing her wit, she remarked, "I began to wonder whether or not he'd ever been in trouble with the law, been married before, or had stinky feet when he removed his combat boots, after he'd put his best foot forward, of course! Turned out the answer was 'yes' to all my questions. I wish I'd known how he treated his former wife and women in general. I wish I'd known what kind of animal he'd choose to own. I didn't have to wonder long about what role he had played in his neighborhood as a child, or what kind of animal he'd own, since we were soon the proud owners of a Doberman named 'Bully.'"

The dog died while the big sergeant was overseas on military duty, but Saige was terrified to write and tell him. "A veterinarian told me Bully had cancer, and after being ill for a few months the dog died. I never told the sergeant what had happened until he came home. I sent the kids to a neighbor's home while I told him. He was so furious that he screamed all night long, reminding me over and over that he'd invested thousands of dollars in the dog for kennel and shipping charges, cosmetic surgery, and obedience training. He should have enrolled in the training too, maybe he could have gotten a two-for-one deal. Big weighed over 300 pounds at that time, so I just listened quietly and said nothing when he accused me of being jealous of the dog and injecting him with a cancer serum! Can you believe it? I was so afraid of that dog I wouldn't get any closer than I had to when I fed him. Give him a shot? I don't think so.

"No doubt about it, Big, as I called him in my mind, was the meanest son-of-a-bitch west of the Rockies. I found out that shortly after he joined the service he'd been stabbed in the shoulder by one of his own troops and had singlehandedly destroyed the buddy system in his platoon. While we were married, he was sent to Vietnam. I wrote and asked him if he'd send me a picture of himself that I could show the children so they wouldn't forget him. Well, Big, or 'Father of the Year,' as I sarcastically referred to him at times, sent me a picture of his private parts. I should have used the picture for a dart board, but I burned it instead. Every person who has ever met this guy hates him, sooner or later. I was definitely in the ranks of those who hated him sooner."

Her reflections skipped freely back and forth through the years. "In the first month of our marriage, I had hot spaghetti and chili dinners thrown in my face—which caused blisters—and anything else around the house that he could get his hands on. He called me horrible names and said other very ugly words to me for no reason. I was pregnant with our first child, as I have previously confessed. Before the end of this marriage, I would be the mother of three more children. There was always so much mental anguish, not to mention the physical abuse. I continued to have chairs, phones, books, dinners, keys, snakes, and many other items thrown at me during this marriage. During one tirade he nearly choked me to death. He was sitting on my chest with his knees against my neck. I thought my chest was going to be crushed. It was like trying to fend off King Kong. I couldn't breathe and was teetering between consciousness and unconsciousness. If a neighbor hadn't heard my screams and ran to our house, I would have died. I went to the hospital and x-rays revealed that a few ribs had been broken in addition to cuts and bruises over most of my body. I weighed only 118 pounds—no match for Big.

"I always lied to the doctors and other people, because Big threatened to kill me if I told anyone about the beatings. Another night, the beating began by him slapping me in the face, and escalated to slugging me in the face and trying to crush my nose into my brain. The cries from the children stopped him from finishing me off. Soon after recovering from that beating, he dragged me by my hair in front of company and pulled me around a banquet table by my nose at a gala military affair. I was so embarrassed and humiliated at the military banquet that I wanted to get under the table and scream at the top of my lungs. God bless the colonel who publicly reprimanded him, because the beatings stopped for the remainder of time we were on that post. He publicly humiliated me on so many occasions that it would be impossible to recall all of them. He also pulled Wyatt's hair and did so much damage to his scalp that now, thirty years later, there's still nerve damage to the scalp area. Big left permanent emotional scars on all of us. Our lives were unbearable every day he was home. I'm so sorry my children suffered and are still suffering.

Although I noted some inconsistencies in her tale, such as keeping quiet about the beatings while also talking of public abuse and humiliation, I couldn't doubt that Saige had married a brutal, bullying man, and that, even now, many years later, she found some relief or outlet for her hurts by talking about them even if perhaps somewhat distorting them. I listened with mixed feelings of curiosity, anger, and sadness.

The litany continued. "One Easter Sunday I was beaten with the leg of a foot stool in front of my children. I ended up with a broken eardrum and multiple cuts and bruises, but was able to drive myself to a military hospital in the country where we were stationed. There isn't an Easter Sunday that goes by that I don't think about that horrible beating. I can't begin to tell you about all the meanness that befell me and my children. I found out very soon after the marriage ceremony that there was no pleasing this man. We couldn't do anything right and were always walking on eggshells when he was home. Big was always either beating or insulting some member of our family, unless there was a good sports program on television. We loved it when he was away," she remarked simply.

"Throughout the marriage, Big came first. His job, his bowling, his male friends, his female lovers, his cars, his toys, his privacy, his quiet time, his food, everything. His language was absolutely filthy. It would have made the devil blush! Nothing was ever done to his satisfaction. Of course, he would never help do anything. When he was home, he was either eating, sleeping, watching television, yelling at us, beating us, or embarrassing us in front of other people. I've had my life threatened many times, and many times he beat me so badly he nearly carried out his threats. The children and I waited on him hand and foot. We even ran his bath water and made sure it was the correct temperature. We laid his clothes out for him so he could dress after his bath. We carried his food to him on a tray, because he always ate alone in the recliner in his bedroom. We were his servants and his pissing posts. He never ever had a kind word to say to us. I truly believe his mission in life was to make all of us as miserable as he possibly could. He must have laid awake at nights planning the punishments and cruelties he would carry-out the following day. The cruelty was endless. I really cannot adequately describe the pain and humiliation we endured during those years. I wish I could have found the courage to divorce him when he abused me the first time. I now blame my fears—being pregnant and worrying about not being able to make it on my own, being intimidated because he was several years older than I, having another failed marriage, and the fear of his violent rages and being harmed or killed."

She paused, then continued, "I've asked myself hundreds of times why I didn't leave him. It seems to me that we women are just too willing to accept the responsibility and blame for the poor behavior of others. Certainly, it has to be our fault. What are we doing wrong? How can we make it better? I had envisioned myself killing him on several occasions throughout our marriage, so I went to a psychiatrist for help. He assured me I wasn't crazy and told me that I was only trying to cope and live with this monster. Big was vicious. His behavior caused any friend I ever had to stay away. He called most women sluts and whores. He called me those names on a daily basis.

"At Christmas time, there were always gifts under the tree to him from all of us but never anything for me or the children from him. I always did all of the holiday shopping. Oh please, just one little gift to lift my spirits, I've wished many, many times," she confessed. The man's meanness and brutality were pictured as so great that I'm sure many would protest that she had to be exaggerating. Still, her present circumstances and his basic brutality, even if overstated, caused her suffering which gave her some license—at least to my mind—to find some release in talking about those troubles.

"I had several miscarriages during our marriage," she told me. "During my first miscarriage I started hemorrhaging and Big said to me, 'I'm not going to take you to the hospital, bitch!' Naturally, it was during the night and Big stayed in bed, so I woke up my oldest daughter, Cheyenne, and told her to watch the little ones so I could get some help for myself. I knew the children would be asleep for the next few hours. I drove myself to the hospital and called my neighbor for help. Later, I called the house and asked Big to please bring me my overnight case with a toothbrush and makeup. He said, 'You're not entering any f—ing beauty contest. I won't bring you anything,' and hung up. A nurse gave me the things I needed. I'd been in labor for thirty-six hours when I lost the baby. I didn't see Big until a few days later when he came to take me home. He cursed me the whole way home because he had to bring someone with him to drive my car back home. About two hours later, Big packed his clothes and left. He was still in the army and returned to his duty station, even though he still had a few days of leave left. He could have stayed, but he chose to return. I was left alone with my little ones. I began hemorrhaging the day after he left, so I packed all four kids into my car and drove back to the hospital. The doctors were furious."

Saige continued her recitation without comment from me; but years elapsed and shifted in the narrative without explanation. "Finally, I had to have a hysterectomy, and was relieved for the most part. Big called me at the hospital and said, 'Hey, I don't care if you drop dead, and when it's time for you to come home, find your own way!' Perhaps it had been an unrealistic expectation for him to pick me up— after all, nobody is perfect. This time I was about an hour and a half away from home. I had to call my best friend to come and get me. She had to take time off from work to pick me up. By the time I got home I was in terrible pain, and Big wouldn't fill my prescriptions. Luckily, my church friends stopped by to see how I was doing, and they went downtown and got my prescriptions filled.

"Every morning when I woke up I hoped he would say something nice to me. I finally decided that it wasn't as if I'd let myself go. There were offers coming my way to go out, from men who were both married and not married. I guess others found me attractive. Of course, I never went with any of them, but in a way it was flattering to know that someone thought I was worth being with. Big never found anything positive about me. It was his nature to pick on other people and humiliate them. He had no character. He made fun of every part of my body: my neck, my eyes, my broken nose—he broke it—my face. He cut me down so low I felt like whale shit on the bottom of the ocean.

"We hadn't had much of a sex life for years. I should have known there were other women, but I guess I didn't want to be hurt even more by admitting it. Big went to New York City on business after retiring from the military, and when he returned home he gave me the 'Oscar winning' performance that was suppose to free him forever from having sex with me. Big said to me, 'Oh, by the way, while I was in New York City I bumped into a door in my hotel room and cut my head real bad. I stopped the bleeding and got dressed for my business meeting. Just after I left my hotel room for my meeting downtown, I was walking down the sidewalk to get a taxi, and there was a drug addict who was bleeding from his hand and bumped into my head wound with his bleeding hand. Now I have AIDS, and, in order to protect you, I can never have sex with you again.' For the next four years, until our divorce, the *gentleman* kept his promise to protect me. Yes, be with those who respect you, and whom you respect. What a guy! I've had many a good laugh over his story," she concluded sarcastically.

I was unprepared for the length of time her marriage had lasted. Saige continued: "After twenty-two years of absolute hell, I told him to 'get out.' There wasn't much left of me. He had totally destroyed me. You'd think that he must have done something really horrible to make me call it quits, but, compared to some of his other attacks, it was nothing. One day, as he was leaving on a three-week trip, either for his job or a bowling tournament, I asked him if I could please have twenty-five dollars to pay for the children's piano lessons and school lunches. He cursed me for a few minutes and then made out a check and threw it on the floor. Then he said, 'Now, go crawl for it and pick it up in your teeth, like the dog you are!' He grabbed me by my hair and pulled me toward the check until I reached it and picked it up with my teeth. Suddenly, I realized that this was the last time *this* dog was going to crawl. I'd finally had enough.

"When he came home from his trip, his clothes and possessions were packed and on the front porch. A few hours later he was served divorce papers. Oh, he ranted and raved about what he was going to do to me if I tried to kick him out or wanted any child support. Well, the law told him what he was and wasn't going to do to me and what he was or wasn't going to give me. It has taken ten years to finally pull myself together emotionally and have some peace of mind. My thoughts of him are only negative, because all there ever was from him were negative experiences. There just aren't any good memories. How could there be?" she exclaimed.

"I could tell you hundreds of stories about the abuse my children and I received during this marriage. The important thing is, I finally got the nerve, or guts, to divorce him. I was almost forty-five years old when I threw the bum out. Best move I ever made. I can't believe I let him treat me and the children so badly for all those years. I guess I figured I wasn't strong enough to make it alone. I'm now a grandmother many times over. My five children are grown and have lives of their own. It's been hard on every one of us to forget the cruelty and abuse against us during my marriages," Saige reiterated.

It was a relief to both of us, I believe, when she moved past her abusive husband and continued her tale. "I worked in the administrative field most of my married life and made very good money, but it was never enough. I spent every cent I made, and then some, on my family and our home. All the while, Big was salting away his money in bank accounts. He always made me feel like I wasn't doing enough or pulling my weight financially. He knew which of my buttons to push. He was setting me up for financial disaster, and I failed to recognize what he was doing until it was too late. We had a beautiful lakeside home and he sold it, saying the children should be closer to their schools. He never drove them to their schools, or went to any of their conferences or other school functions. He bought a very cheap, run-down house for me and the children and pocketed the huge equity from the big house. Only a minimum down payment was paid on the house for the kids and me. I ended up having to totally remodel the house, paying for it myself. Then he suddenly decided to retire from the military, just two months shy of the date when I'd be eligible for any military benefits, I later learned. I should have found out more about military retirement to better protect myself and the children. After Big retired, he got jobs that took him away from home three weeks each month. One weekend I decided to surprise him with a visit, so I loaded the kids into our station wagon and drove to the city where he was living. It turned out that we were the ones who got the surprise—we found him naked, with a woman. Again, I should have known there must be others, but I'd chosen not to think about it.

"I've played the game of love and lost," she maintained. "I hadn't known the rules or had the insight to be a winner. Now I've lost all interest in the game, not to mention the prizes. Both husbands broke me, only in different ways, and Big was probably my last hurrah.

"After the divorce, I was doing fine financially. I was working for a major corporation. I'd paid off my home and gotten my children through school, and then the big layoff came. There were so many obligations for me. I started sinking financially ... just couldn't pull things together. My parents were dead and the rest of my family had given me as much as they could; but there had been others I'd helped when they were in need. They were on top of their problems and could've thrown me a lifeline until I could turn things around for myself. I know we're not supposed to expect anything in return when we help others, but I was in desperate need."

I had to imagine her support system, her needs, as she did not dwell on her own financial missteps, or whatever it was that caused her financial ruin. Like most of us, she was better at, or more comfortable with, reciting the failures or shortcomings of others. She continued abruptly with the recitation of her sufferings and her response to them. "I began to sell my furniture off, piece by piece. When my piano went out the door, I cried and cried. My daddy had bought it for me years before, because he knew how much I loved music. I played for the choir at our church, for funerals, weddings, accompaniments for soloists, and for other events. I played for hours on end to calm my mind. I used to call it the best nerve pill in the world. It was almost like losing a family member. I sold it to pay my house taxes. I was also helping my children with their financial needs. Finally, I lost my home. I've been accused by others of not being good-hearted but fool-hearted for giving away my life, my possessions, my money, and as a result, have destroyed myself both personally and financially. I couldn't see it back then."

She stated that she had tried to find a job, with no results, claiming, "God only knows how many places I've gone on interviews." She took charge of her grandson because her daughter was going to put him into a foster home or up for adoption because she felt she just couldn't raise him because of his neurological condition and hyperactivity. "I felt I could not give up my own flesh and blood, so I'm raising him. It would be so much easier for me if I only had myself to worry about. I'm homeless and destitute. Why now, at this stage in my life, with a grandson to raise?" she asked, receiving, and probably expecting, no answer from me.

Saige's next words gave a valuable key to her character, revealing that she was not just a weak woman of little will. Though I believe that is in part true, it was more complicated. "I've always tried to hang in there and not quit. Anyone in their right mind would have given up on my two disastrous marriages much sooner than I did, but family values and a determination not to fail probably kept me in there. I kept trying until all hope was gone. When I was at my lowest and weakest condition, I received lots of advice from people about what to do. I'm sure they meant well. However, I was too ill to put their words

into action. I've always remembered what John F. Kennedy said that
fit my situation perfectly: 'If we are strong, our character will speak
for itself. If we are weak, words will be of no help.'

"Prior to coming here to Las Vegas and to this shelter, my grandson and I were living at my oldest daughter's home. There was no
work in the area, so we were forced to leave. I packed mine and Will's
belongings into my old car and headed out of town. I had no job, no
insurance, no bank account, plenty of bills, and Will and I were both
ill. I didn't know how far we'd get, but I hoped to find a job before my
car broke down or we ran out of gas money." Although she "felt overwhelmed" by the situation, desperation had driven her to flight.

Saige looked around the shelter, realizing what she must do, and
said, "Once again, I have to start a new life. When little Will and I were
about to run out of gas and our pocket change was gone, we located
this shelter. I was so tired that I wondered if I had the strength to find
a place to park the car and get us through the door." She expressed
gratitude for the medical help they had received, but then said, "I'm
worried, and wonder what will happen to little Will if I should die.
Here I am, in a shelter, when once I owned a beautiful home. I had to
come here to find people who cared enough to save my life. They've
already given us shelter, free medicines, food, clothing, eyeglasses, and
hope. I've lived in neighborhoods full of big homes where many of the
people living there didn't even know my name, let alone help me.
Maybe there's a lesson for me to learn from my homelessness. I see so
many homeless, lonely, sad people here, especially women over fifty. It
scares me to death. I can now relate, because I'm one of them. If I ever
make it back to where I can help a shelter or rescue mission, believe
me, I will take whatever I can to them so they can continue to help
others in need," she affirmed.

Saige was a woman obviously trying to get back on her feet, having a sense of purpose to go with her natural endurance, and hoping
to find the energy—and helping hand—to continue. She summed up
her situation, "My spirits are better now. I refuse to succumb to my
present situation or my fears. I have too much to live for. Raising my
grandson is going to be a tremendous responsibility, but I will give
him the best childhood I can.... We may be homeless at the moment,
but it's only a temporary thing. I've learned lessons from my marriages and losses, and from now on I'm going to live a more simple
life. I'm just going to accept things the way they are and not try to fix

them. I'm not going to wish things were different or try to mend what's beyond repair—not people, not relationships. I will no longer march to the beat of unreasonable orders or demands from anyone else."

In retrospect, reviewing my recordings of our conversations, I still believe that there was much that was incongruous in her tale and situation; but I now believe that some of her surprisingly more polished language—although it was mixed with a great deal of profanity—was consciously used by her to try to gain my respect and that of the readers of this book. Though some of it seemed unnatural, it did indicate her education and perhaps that most natural desire of all: to favorably impress those we encounter.

Saige ended her story by saying, "If I could leave a message to the young girls just starting out in life, it would be that no one else is probably going to rescue you from your poor decisions. Sometimes they can't. Keep yourself in a position where you won't need to be rescued. Be responsible. Be self-sufficient. Do not settle. Become self-confident. Learn to recognize if something is worthwhile in the beginning. You do have choices. Get to know your partner before you marry. Is he husband and father material? Don't ever put yourself in a position where you have to get married. No one is happy in a trap! I haven't had a life of my own since my teenage years, but I'd like one now. My children are all grown and have lives of their own now, except for little Will. I must rise above my current situation and stand up for one last time if I'm going to regain my place in society and earn the respect of others."

Cecily ━━━━━━━━━━━━━━━━━━━━━━━━━━

Eᴀʀʟʏ ᴏɴᴇ ᴍᴏʀɴɪɴɢ in April 1995 I arrived at the Dallas Life Foundation Building in Dallas, Texas. People of every description were mingling outside, either waiting for someone to pick them up or waiting to enter the building. Most of them were talking about the terrible event that had happened the day before. There was a lot of panic in the Dallas-Fort Worth area in the wake of the bombing of the Alfred E. Murrah Federal Building in Oklahoma City, which was located about 200 miles away. Law enforcement investigators were conducting searches around Dallas because there had been reports that some of the participants in the bombing might be in the area. Before entering the day resource center, everyone had to state their business and pass through a security detection system; however, I learned this was standard procedure and not a result of the bombing incident.

After being cleared to enter, I was introduced to the assistant director and explained my purpose for coming to the center. I asked his permission to interview one of the women currently "in-house" about her homelessness. He was most pleasant and helpful and told me that he'd ask around to see if anyone was interested. He gave me permission to use his office should there be a woman who consented to an interview. I had only waited about ten minutes when he returned and introduced me to a homeless woman named Cecily.

Cecily was a shy, good-looking, thirty-nine-year-old black woman, dressed in an attractive pink dress. She was thin and stately, and she carried a black umbrella, a book, sunglasses, and a handkerchief in her hands. Her hair was swept back and held to her head by a fashionable pink and silver clip. She smiled demurely as she sat down in a chair directly across from me, promptly apologizing for the way she looked. "My dress is a bit wrinkled, but it's clean. If I'd known about being interviewed, I'd have spent more time on my hair."

I assured her that she looked very nice, which she did.

Cecily bowed her head and nervously folded and refolded the handkerchief in her lap. Her account began quietly and seriously. She spoke in a low, soft voice as she began the story of her homelessness, which resulted from a series of problems that only gradually became revealed in the course of the account. As usual, I sat and listened, only occasionally asking questions or making brief comments to bring some coherence and order to the story. I later tried to arrange it in a basic chronological order, where possible. She actually began abruptly telling of her troubles prior to and just after a divorce, perhaps seeing them as the direct cause of her homelessness and trying to accommodate my desire to learn about causes of homelessness.

Cecily shared the days of her childhood. "I was a spiritual child, raised by my daddy in the Church of Christ. My belief in prayer was strong and I was always trying to save my family, it seems. I knew there was something wrong with our family. In church we were taught to honor our father and mother, but I was confused by my mother's actions. She never went to church or anywhere else with us if she could get out of it, preferring not to be a part of our family at all. She was always so ugly to us. I didn't know it at the time, but I was soon going to be called a 'poor motherless child' by the people in our town. One day our momma's tongue was flappin', and she told us, 'I've decided to leave home and become a nurse. I can't stay here any longer if I'm going to better myself and live the life of my dreams. You are all a hindrance to me. I'm not about to miss out.' I wondered how momma could nurse others, when she couldn't even nurse her own.

"After momma left, daddy said he was better off without her. I don't know what he ever saw in her in the first place … her complexion, I guess. Daddy told momma before she left, 'take those children with you; it's not that I'd neglect them, but you need to learn how to be a mother.' She told him that she didn't want any of us with her in her new life. I heard daddy tell her, 'keeping the children together means everything to me, so if you won't take care of them, I will!' She said, 'then you can do the raisin' up.' A woman has to be messed up to do what momma did. She was, and still is, an empty person. Nobody home. Different.

"Time passed and we never saw momma. Then one day out of nowhere we got a phone call from her. She said, 'I've been diagnosed with throat cancer, and would you all take pity and pray for me? I only have six months to live.' Well, we all went to church regularly and prayed and prayed for her, even though she'd mistreated us all so badly. With treatment and all our prayers, she recovered and soon returned to her old ways. It tests a person's character to turn the other cheek," Cecily reflected. She then resumed her story with little prodding from me.

"Daddy passed on when I was but thirteen years old, and it was to be the turning point in my life. I was grateful for the love and guidance he'd given us children, and missed him beyond belief. He'd taught us right from wrong and to live by the Ten Commandments and the Golden Rule. The experiences we shared together after our parents divorced were better than living with the ugliness and wondering what was going on in our home. My parents just didn't agree on what they wanted to do as separate individuals. Knowing that daddy was gone now caused some real fright in me. I remember how hard I'd wished that I could have just one more talk with him to hear his words of wisdom and encouragement. Just one more smile to make me feel that everything would be all right and that I was loved by someone. I was hurting deep inside and was no longer in the arms of the safety my daddy had provided for me.

"I was supposed to stay with relatives, you know, but I figured since I had a mother I could stay with her. Well, my mother thought she needed us children like a submarine needed a screen door. She's not the same type of person I am. I was more of a real woman at thirteen than she was at whatever her age. To me, a real woman is someone who can handle her own; she doesn't worry about another woman outdoing her, and she takes care of her husband, her children, and her home. The things momma said and did shocked me. She didn't care if some other woman came along and took her husband and her children. We just didn't exist in her heart. There wasn't warmth nor bond to be had between mother and children. My greatest wish was to be in my mother's home, in a warm safe bed, and have her smile at me. This was not to be. After daddy died, momma wanted me to play adult games, but I wasn't ready for prime time. The games she played with me were ones that tried to force me into motherhood just to keep me out of her life. I told her that I didn't want to get married, just wanted to finish school and get a good job.

"I was one of those intuitive kids while growing up. If I could sense something was wrong in our family, I tried to fix it. I didn't have to be told there was a problem, I just knew.... If it was money we needed, I went out and got a small job. I helped my daddy any way I could. Everything that girls do at a young age, I was doing. I was just that type of person. I had a fight or two with other kids, because I was trying to fit in with the crowd.

"Momma didn't want any of us children in her adult home, and so I finally realized that the time had come for me to be on my own. Momma had 'swept out the charm' on some poor Christian fellow and he'd married her. She now had a beautiful home and was a nurse, so her dreams had been realized. I'd show her, I thought. I moved in with a group of the wrong type of kids—the kind who wanted to experience everything all at once. I really didn't want to live like that and wanted to leave, so I called momma, again, and begged her to let me live with her. She refused. I wanted to finish school more than anything and have a mother, but finally understood that momma was not ever going to help me or be there when I needed her." Since Cecily hadn't said, it wasn't clear where her siblings stayed after her father's death.

"I was young and confused, but I understood what momma was trying to do. She had tried to make me believe that my way of thinking was wrong, but I knew better. I couldn't see how quitting school and getting married would lead me to the place where I wanted to be. What a hypocrite she was! I remember how she hadn't wanted to miss her opportunity for an education. She'd given up everything, including me. A young girl shouldn't have to give up her childhood and young adulthood before its time. Marriage plans should be discussed in great detail after meeting the man you want to spend your life with and father your children. Well, honey, I finally stopped fighting momma and hurried up and got pregnant. She was more like my enemy than my mother, and she'd just won the battle: the doctor had confirmed that I was pregnant.

"Momma was happy at last! She found my brother and told him to go out and rent a church and make arrangements for what was supposed to be one of the happiest days of my life. I knew I would need plenty of inner strength and courage to carry off this happy event! My feet got cold the morning of the wedding and wouldn't go to the church. Momma was furious and came to the place where I was staying, and was even more furious when I was still in my robe! She said, 'Cecily, get ready and get to the church, you've got to get married!' I said, 'No, I don't!' Seemed like momma always got her way, though, and I went to church that morning and was married. Everything I'd ever wanted for myself also went that morning. I hoped my daddy wasn't watching me on this particular day, but, remembering back, I'm sure the reason it was raining outside was because the heavens were weeping. He wouldn't have wanted to give me away to the kind of man I married, under any circumstance," Cecily said, as she finished talking about her wedding-day blues.

Cecily then began the account of this new phase of her life, also an unhappy one, as it turned out. "My lot in life was very hard to accept. I was full of despair for a lot of reasons and knew full well this wasn't what I wanted. I'd let myself down. I hadn't kept my Christian commandments and thought I was being punished for this. I couldn't finish my education. I'd settled for an older man I didn't really want and who wasn't even my kind or kind to me. I'd sold my dreams down the river ... 'all out of pleasing,' in every sense of the phrase. I'd only been an inconvenience to my mother. My self-worth was exceedingly low during this period. I was so depressed that I didn't get out of bed for a whole month."

Numerous years of a life can be brushed aside as one focuses on their conclusion. So it was with Cecily's account of her marriage. "My husband and I divorced after ten years of marriage, but some good came to me during the marriage, too. I had two fine sons, earned my General Education Diploma and had a good job. My husband's actions throughout our entire marriage caused me great anguish, and I'd wondered many times if I'd always have to stay with him or would there be some way out for me. After suffering mental abuse for years, I couldn't take it any longer and was forced to seek a divorce. I wasn't ending my marriage only for myself, I also wanted my boys raised as good Christians, rather than being around someone who had no values. My husband was an alcoholic, irrational, and a womanizer. Count them—three strikes. There were more than a few moments in my marriage when I believed that I'd had enough, but I wasn't prepared for the actual happening of a divorce and finding out that nothing would ever be the same for me again. I couldn't stand to be around all the negative behavior, you know, and my man didn't want to change a thing to make our marriage better. I had just wanted to be treated like a lady, taken to dinner, and receive a little present every now and again," Cecily declared. At this point, she looked up a little sheepishly and said, "Please don't think I'm selfish. I finally realized that I'd married too young, to a man I didn't want, and we had nothing in common."

Cecily stared at nothing in particular for a few moments and then said, "His womanizing still amazes me. He thought he was slick and wouldn't get caught, but all the while he was destroying his relationship with the boys and me, his friends, and others. I wanted to tell his women, 'Gol darn girl, don't try to get my man if he treats me and his children right and helps us with our burdens. If he's just using me and is helping you with your burdens, and is mistreating me and our children badly, there's no fairness.' My man just wanted his own way and meant to continue … well, not with me! I'd rather be single than settle for the crumbs and ugliness he was dishing out. I just needed to have the means to keep going. I liked to dress well. I liked to stay home at night with my boys. I'm not a party person. I love a guy who gives of himself and treats his family right, so being mistreated and used the way I was hadn't set well with me. Even though our marriage was rocky from the start, I'd decided early on that I was going to do my best to make the marriage work; but my decision couldn't stand the tests of time and good judgment.

"I tried to cope with my problems the best I could, but about eight years ago my world finally fell apart. Late at night when it was quiet, my thoughts raced and were really loud; my face would burn, and I'd sometimes have to slap my face to try and focus my attention away from my thoughts. I didn't want to act this way. Dwelling only on the negative wasn't good for me, but I couldn't help it. I couldn't come out of my house, either, and wondered if there would ever be an end to my sorry behavior. I was barely making it through each day, and, with no sleep, my recovery was falling behind. After my boys left for school each morning, I'd just cry and scream, hour after hour. Most days I stayed in bed until noon. When I did get up, I'd spend the rest of the day running from one chore to the next. I couldn't sit down for long and would do my tasks over and over again. It was frightening to be this low and out of control. The realities of my life were hard to face, and going to work was just out of the question—just couldn't do it. I was traveling on a bad road with no end in sight, and it seemed to be leading to nothing but more misery. Even though I knew I couldn't continue in my marriage, I wasn't prepared for the trauma that had resulted from the divorce and breakup of my family. The reality of my actual divorce left me unable to function, paralyzing me with anxiety and grief that seemed to be neverending."

Remembering her life immediately after her divorce was difficult for Cecily, but she spoke of her feelings and actions during that time. "I kept thinking … my life isn't supposed to be this way. I need to go back to work and make money and do the things I've always done. It would make a big difference, most definitely, and interaction with other people would be good for me and keep my mind off my troubles. But I just couldn't do it. Each day was just like the day before. It took the best in me and all my power to keep on going. Every person has a limit to the trouble and stress they can endure, and believe me, honey, I'd met mine! I'd gone up one hill after another all my life, but I couldn't climb any longer. This was not the hill I wanted to die on, but maybe I would anyway. I was getting worse and worse and prayed constantly to God for help, but felt that maybe He had other plans for me since my condition wasn't improving.

"I'd lost my job after my husband and I divorced because the stress it caused in my life left me unable to function. I'd tried to hang on and pay the bills, take care of the boys, take care of the house, and work full-time, but I just couldn't do it all. Also, my husband and I worked at the same place, and I found it unbearable to be so close to him. I'd done well during the eight years I'd worked there and had excellent performance evaluations. Finally, though, I'd used all my leave time and still couldn't go to work … so I was let go. Eventually, I lost everything and my life's been destroyed," Cecily said, sorrowfully, "and I can't seem to put it all back together." Years had passed in that brief account, without any details being supplied as to how Cecily had "lost everything." That was undoubtedly the result, however. I listened for more information.

Returning to the present, she said, "There are so many mornings I wake up and say to myself, 'Cecily, why are you sleeping under the stars, girl? Look at your circumstances. I can't believe you've gotten us homeless. What are we doing here on this bench—alone, middle-aged, with good senses and mind, a nice figure, and good looking? Enough is enough. Get a going.' But, I'll tell you what—I'm bitter. I've lived on the streets for eight years now and have endured many hardships. I really tried hard while growing up to be the best person I could be, but was rejected by my own mother. This is not to be expected in nature's scheme of things. During my youth I couldn't figure out why momma didn't like any of us. I tried hard to please her, but couldn't. Most of my troubles today are because of her. I had good values and lived right, but the right opportunities didn't come along for me."

Cecily proclaimed, "One day I'm gonna tell momma, 'Momma, you put me on the hill, but I only got a flesh wound and didn't die. Your advice stunk! My life would have been so different if you'd even met me halfway.'"

I was puzzled how Cecily spent her days, so I asked. She replied, "Books are a joyous escape from my homeless life. I love reading about the adventures and pleasurable lives of other people, and spend many hours each day in city libraries. I have a library card that I treasure. A friend helped me get it. I always dress nicely and carry my backpack with me, so I'm thought of as a student of sorts. That way, I can stay as long as I want and no one bothers me. On many mornings when I awake and find out I'm still alive, I immediately begin reading a book. Some days I read a whole book and don't even bother eating until the sun goes down. My favorite author is Maya Angelou, and I especially like her book that I have with me today, *I Know Why the Caged Bird Sings*. She writes about the things I'm interested in and am somewhat familiar with—difficult childhoods. There are some words in the book that answer a lot of questions for me."

"Find those words in your book and share them with me," I requested. Cecily read:

> All of childhood's unanswered questions must finally be passed back to [one's hometown] and answered there. Heroes and bogey men, values and dislikes, are first encountered and labeled in that early environment. In later years they change faces, places and maybe races, tactics, intensities and goals, but beneath those penetrable masks they wear forever the stocking-capped faces of childhood.

After reading the wisdom of Maya Angelou, Cecily said, "I'm not alone in my way of thinking, after all."

"How do you take care of your personal needs, Cecily?" I asked her. "I shower and put clean clothes on here at the center each morning," she replied. "I wash my things at my friends' places or in laundromats. I leave here and go to the 'Stew Pot' to eat. It's a place where street people gather to eat and visit with each other. These people are truly great for me, and the longer I'm with them the more I want to stay with them. We do a lot of junk talking, which I enjoy immensely. I laugh with them and appreciate the friendliness directed toward me. I've stopped being so negative in my thinking, you know, because when I first met them they told me, 'Cecily, you have a serious attitude problem, girl, and if it's a good job and a stable life you want, well then, you're going to have to change your attitude.' They're like family to me. I keep telling myself that I need to look forward to my future and that it's dangerous for me to feel too comfortable in my homeless lifestyle if it's my goal to get off the streets. I then force myself to leave my street friends and look for a job. I work out of temporary employment services and they send me to jobs at car washes and other places. I haven't made much money, but it's money I can call my own. I can buy things for myself or go out for the day to see a movie—it's so relaxing. I can do these things, though, only after I've earned money for them. I really enjoy working with people."

Cecily then told me more about her daily life and routine as a homeless person. Some parts of this recitation were not so pleasant and, in fact, could be quite terrifying. "I start getting anxious in the late afternoon, because I know that the time has come to once again find a safe place to sleep. I see the homeless sleeping in tents, under cardboard boxes, in sleeping bags, under ragged blankets, under garbage, in thick bushes, or just out in the open with nothing on them. I once believed that tents and sleeping bags were only found at the circus or used when camping. Myself, I have an old sleeping bag and blanket and try to find an empty bench somewhere, usually on the grounds of my church. I prefer to stay by myself, however, because I've had a few bad experiences around others after dark.

"I remember one night in particular,… while I was looking for a spot to sleep on the church grounds, a wild-eyed, hairy, animal-like man approached me and said, 'Hello, doll face, do you need some company?' I could smell liquor on his breath and he really frightened me. He grabbed me by the arm and I pulled away. I kept calm and told him that my friends were waiting for me inside the church, but I'd see him when the service was over. That response seemed to satisfy him. I quickly entered the church, which was always open. I kept peeking out a window to see if the man was still there and saw that he never left the front door. I finally decided to go out the back door and hide in some thick bushes all night. There wasn't room for me to move around or lie down in them because they were full of stickers, which reminded me not to move. My legs were cramping every now and again, but I didn't dare move because I feared the man might still be out there in the dark and hear me. As the night progressed, I became more and more disgusted with myself for being homeless, and thought, 'Do I like living like this? I must, because I do it every night, year after year. Am I crazy? Maybe so. What's wrong with me?' Just before dawn a pack of big dogs roamed the church grounds and were sniffing around in some bushes close by. I thought for sure they'd give me away, but they didn't, and soon left. Suddenly, it occurred to me that I'd crawled into the bushes on 'all fours,' just like the prowling dogs," Cecily said, adding, "I guess all homeless people are somewhat like animals after living on the streets for any length of time."

"Was the man you feared still on the church grounds when morning came?" I asked her.

"No," she answered.

Cecily was at the mercy of the streets, and realized it. "The street people can see the church bus coming and going all through the night as it picks up and drops off the homeless for whatever help they need. It's kind of comforting to see that someone else is up all night long, too. People who've never been homeless take so many things for granted. I'll bet they've never wondered where to go for a midnight snack, a drink of water, or a bathroom call during the night. If they get sick there is medicine in a cabinet. Not being able to locate their house slippers is probably their biggest concern. I haven't owned a pair in years."

Cecily continued to talk, alternating between comments on her present lifestyle, reflections on homelessness in general, and reminiscences from her past. "I attend church services regularly and enjoy fellowshipping with everyone. I especially love to hear the sermons and sing the hymns. My church 'rocks' on Sunday morning as we sing at the top of our voices. It's great! Going to church is like weekend counseling and group therapy in ways, except God is my counselor. In other words, it's very good for me," Cecily affirmed.

"Many homeless women are afraid to be alone and will seek out a man to stay with them for protection and companionship," she told me. "I know how dangerous the streets are and I feel fear during the night; however, I'm a woman who still possesses enough strength, beliefs, and good sense not to settle for 'one night stands.' I thank the

Lord for this strength and wisdom. Some women are not as strong as I am in this respect," she said proudly.

Cecily shook her head in reflection and said, "I'm still shocked every once in a while when I wake up and find myself sleeping outdoors. I wonder if when I live in a house I'll wake up shocked that I'm sleeping there. I stare straight up at the sky when I first wake up, and then look around. Sometimes I can't believe its really me on the park bench, and wonder what I'm doing there. If anyone sees me who knows me, or learns about me, I feel so degraded. This really isn't me, I tell myself. What are people going to think of me? It isn't me,… but it is me. I worry about my sanity sometimes. I've been told in counseling classes to write a journal or dairy about my experiences, but I just can't bring myself to do it. Maybe writing it down on paper would make it real."

There was a pause of a few moments, so I asked Cecily what she needed most but did not have because she lived on the streets. "I'm not going to focus on the negative and things I don't have. Most of my needs are met," she replied. "The homeless outreach vans come and take me to Parkland Hospital if I need medical attention, and there are food kitchens like the Stew Pot where I can go to eat. I get my clothing at thrift stores, and I receive counseling at the center. Most important, I can come here to the Life Center and mingle with others and clean up each morning. I don't feel good about being on all these programs, but if a homeless woman, like myself, decides she wants to live the lifestyle, she can survive on the streets," Cecily answered matter-of-factly.

Cecily had a pensive expression on her face as she said, "In conversations with myself, I say, 'Cecily, you'd better get yourself a job! Aren't you tired of feeling worthless and second-class? Haven't you been alone long enough, and faced enough dangers? Do you just want to vanish from society and live in this homeless world forever? You're not nameless. Only your lifestyle has been taken away from you, not your soul. You still have what it takes, girl! It's just buried under eight years of non-use.' 'Cecily girl, you carry yourself very well, even though you're without a home you still look great,' the street people tell me. 'Thank you,' I reply.

"I've tried to maintain my dignity, even though at times it's been hard to pull off. I can't waste my life much longer, though, and must soon begin again. I'm paralyzed to some extent by different fears. I know that I've got to forget about what other people think of me. I also know that if I don't do something soon to get off the streets that I could stay in this depressed state forever," Cecily said honestly. She smiled shyly and continued, 'Take one step out at a time, even if it's only a small step—and don't look backward, look forward,' is what my counselors tell me to do."

She abruptly proclaimed, "I want to get on with the new life I've dreamed about, and I know it would help me if I shared my wants and needs with others so they can help me find a job or a contact to pursue. I need at least one stable base in my life from which I can begin again. I feel that a job and more education will do that for me."

The office lent to us to conduct the interview was suddenly getting very busy. The phones had started to ring, a mailman was delivering mail, staff members were coming in for files, and I didn't want to impose any longer on the important business being done at the center. Cecily and I decided that we'd close our interview with some final comments from her about getting off the streets. She wrapped up her plans for the future, saying, "My counselors tell me that I'm a very nice lady and shouldn't be in this situation; but I am. I know that I'll have to be strong to achieve my goals and must also come to terms about being embarrassed and shy about reentering the mainstream of life. I am where I am today because of the choices I've made, and so now I must choose to get my place back. I want to travel, and I don't mean hitchhiking or jumping on trains like I've done in the past. I shudder now just remembering the last few years and some of the bad characters I've met and the dangerous things I've done. It just wasn't me. I lost my way for a while—quite a while, it seems. In my future, I see a table set with fine china and plates filled with meals fixed by me, a bank account, responsibility, security, health insurance, family get-togethers, comfort, money for my boys, and, yes, a home. I would like to be remembered as an intelligent woman. I'll always want God to walk by my side. He will direct me. Having Him with me is the only way I can, and have, made it on the streets. I don't like being afraid.

"My advice for avoiding homelessness? Get a good education, don't hang out with bad people, stay away from drugs and alcohol and all other negatives. Live a spiritual lifestyle. Amen," Cecily finished, with bowed head and eyes closed.

Jolene ══════════════════════════════

I CALLED A SALVATION ARMY women's shelter in Chattanooga, Tennessee, one morning and spoke to a supervisor about interviewing one of the homeless women staying there. She reminded me of an aunt of mine, a saintly woman who genuinely loved helping others. The sweet lady informed me, "My dear, there's a woman named Jolene currently staying in-house, and she might consent to an interview. The poor dear is feeling very poorly, though, both in body and spirit. I'll speak with her concerning your request."

When I called the shelter later, I was told that Jolene had agreed to an interview in two days providing she could get out of bed. She was experiencing alcohol withdrawal and the impending birth of a child. It may be appropriate to remark here that many homeless women did not want to be interviewed and that those who did cannot necessarily be considered representative (at least in some respects) of most women on the streets. They provided me a great deal of information, but I probably met with some of the more cooperative and friendly women, those who for whatever reason wanted to share their stories. More hostile or less accessible people do not often share their stories with interviewers like me.

As I approached the shelter for the interview, I noticed a strange sight. A single black cloud hung directly over the shelter. There were no other clouds in the sky. Was it a bad omen? I entered the shelter and found my way to where Jolene was staying. An attendant told me, "Jolene isn't quite ready for her interview, so you'll have to wait a few minutes. That's her yelling and singing in the showers in the next room. She's feeling much better today and acting wilder than she has of late."

94

The attendant informed me that Jolene had been upset because she couldn't have alcohol for breakfast, and instructed me to call for a staff member if Jolene got out-of-hand with me.

I could hear Jolene singing, even including stage screams: "Momma with a blue dress, blue dress, blue dress, momma, you devil, put it on! Momma goin' to party soon, party soon, momma goin' to get it on!" Although I recognized the music as a Mitch Ryder and the Detroit Wheels song called "Devil With a Blue Dress On," Jolene had changed some of the words to fit her mood. There was silence for a few minutes, and then, quite suddenly, Jolene came through the swinging doors into the hall where I was waiting for her. Her brown hair was wet and her eyes were red and wild-looking. She wore no makeup and her complexion was sallow. She was dressed in a pair of well-worn maternity jeans and an extra large T-shirt displaying a large rosebud. She made a definitely not-to-be-forgotten first impression.

I was surprised, to say the least, when Jolene's slow walk turned into a slow shuffle. She began rhythmically snapping her fingers as she strolled and boogied toward me. I'd been told she wasn't feeling up to par, but she gave new meaning to the phrase, "put your best foot forward." She acted as though she was at an audition. After seeing her dance, I sensed that what I'd heard about her was true.

Jolene was still standing when she began singing: "Fee fee fie fie fo fo fum, lookin' mighty nice, here she comes; wearin' a wig, hat and shades to match, high-heeled sneakers and an alligator hat. Wearin' her pearls and a diamond ring, bracelets on her fingers and everything." I was truly amazed and with a lot of enthusiasm said, "You should be on stage somewhere, you zany woman! You can really sing. What are you doing here?"

"Somebody poked me!" Jolene answered in a deadpan voice, seemingly resenting the child she was carrying.

I thought she had a terrific voice. It had an earthy, sexy, throaty, quality to it—something like the voice of Dusty Springfield. She smiled and teased me, saying, "Who'd you expect ... Venus in blue jeans? Am I everything you'd hoped I'd be?"

I was speechless and didn't answer her questions. I thought to myself that it was too bad Jolene hadn't used her voice to sing her way to success. Jolene requested that her picture not be taken, because, in her own words, "I look like forty miles of bad road. I'm a wild lookin' and actin' thing that's been penned up for way too long!"

Jolene revealed a reason why she hadn't made a success of her singing career: "I've worked in clubs before, but just couldn't seem to make it to work on time. I was singin' with a good black vocal group for a while, and even though I'm white they accepted me and we got along great. We sounded really good together, too. We called ourselves The Zebras. 'Devil' was the first song we'd do for folks. It's my favorite song." She suddenly put both hands under her belly and began to sing again: "Devil with a blue dress, blue dress, blue dress, devil with a blue dress on!…" finishing another verse of the song.

As suddenly as Jolene's energy had peaked, it evaporated; however, she still wanted to tell her story. Before the attendant left the room, Jolene begged her, "Please, lady, is there somethin' you can do to stop my tremblin' and sick stomach? I'm startin' to shake like a racoon up a tree with twenty hounds a barkin' at it! Can they take the baby now, so I can have another drink?" The attendant replied, "Jolene, you keep on testing me. You know you can't have alcohol, and we're not taking the baby now or it will be shaking too."

Jolene resigned herself to the fact that she would not get the kind of favor she'd requested. After resting a few minutes, she began her story. "Before comin' here, I remember wakin' up down by the Tennessee River and feelin' like I was 'bout to die. The sickness was caused by my long nights of drinkin' with men, and playin' pool and havin' some brewskies with my lady friends, which I plan on doin' again when I get outa here. After hittin' the streets and gettin' my first 'eye opener' of the day, I'm fine again. If I feel a little under the weather, I usually go to a library where no one will bother me. I just get me a book and go to a long table and sit there for hours. Pretendin' to read is easy, just turn a page every now and again. But I have to remember to 'stay awake in class,' or the lady in charge will ask me to leave. Sometimes my eyes won't stay open after a good beatin', and I wear my dark glasses so nobody can see my black eyes. Since I'm expectin' its not been so easy to party and have fun."

Jolene's rapid-fire approach—whether totally natural to her or in part meant to impress me as her audience—needless to say, caught me off guard. Certainly one wouldn't expect to find this boisterous attitude in a homeless shelter. She even included jokes in her stories: "One night at a bar a guy asked me a question I didn't know how to answer, so he slugged me really hard on my arm. He'd asked me, 'Do you know what food women eat that makes 'em lose their sexual desire?' I told him that I didn't know and didn't care, so he hit me and sneered, 'You don't have to worry about eatin' it, though, 'cause you'll never have any of it.' The answer I hadn't known about was 'weddin' cake.' I thought that was a really mean thing to say to me. The other guys a sittin' in our booth just laughed at it all. I hope that someday a guy will ask me to marry him and give me a nice home to live in. Maybe wishin' doesn't have much power behind it, but it's all that keeps me a goin' sometimes." That statement indicated to me that there was a great deal of bravado in her banter. She went on to tell me about aspects of her life as a homeless person.

"Most of the time I sleep down by the river, but durin' the winter I try to find myself a shelter if I'm sober. I know where there's a couple of abandoned shacks, but mostly crackheads or other dangerous guys stay there, so I hide a little farther upstream. The river is my friend. I wash myself and my clothes in it, but I don't drink it 'cause it will rust my pipes! The sound it makes helps me fall asleep. I know the river area pretty well and can hide if I'm afraid of somebody. I most likely will hide in the bushes now, 'cause I can't climb trees like I used to. You probably guessed by now that I can't afford to get a motel room downtown or rent a place. Some days I just sleep and sleep, tryin' to forget my troubles, but a person can only do that for so long.

"One day last fall when I came back to the river from uptown I noticed the garbage bags that I kept my clothes and other things in had been moved. I went over to check on 'em and found out the bags were full of manure and my things were missin'. Some good-for-noth-ing jokers probably thought it was really funny. Wasn't that a labor of love? Well, I lost everything I had in this whole world. I kept hopin' they'd bring my stuff back to me, but they never did. I felt like jumpin' in the river and drownin' myself; but no one would care, so I didn't do it," Jolene said, showing signs of defeat, but still with an attitude of some defiance.

Looking more closely at Jolene, I saw a woman with a sagging spirit in a traumatized body. She'd entered a crossroads in her life, whether she realized it or not. Her alcoholic addiction must soon be left behind, because it seemed to me that she had reached the point of no return. I thought about her helpless unborn child, who would soon have much to face after taking it's first breath. She looked so ill, and her eyes appeared to be drained of hope. I'm sorry to say this, but she looked somewhat ghoulish. When she wasn't "on stage" she was almost a non-person, if that's possible. She had a vacant stare in her eyes and would raise and lower them in a manner than was unsettling to me. I asked her if she felt well enough to continue our interview, and she said that she did. She told me to be patient with her, because she'd sang and danced herself out of energy and was shaking from her withdrawal from alcohol.

Defiance and bitterness were evident in her next words: "I don't especially care 'bout helpin' others by tellin' 'em my story ... let 'em find out for themselves. Maybe they'll like the way I live my life. Truth is, the folks here are tryin' to dry me out before this baby is born, which will be any day now. I can't forget 'bout the drinks though.... First thing I want every mornin' is a drink. If I wasn't in this place, I'd get me one 'cause it makes me feel better. Some folks tell me I shouldn't drink before noon or I'll be an alcoholic, but I just tell 'em that it's always noon somewhere in the world!" Jolene then laughed raucously, justifying her feelings and needs. She wasn't telling me anything I hadn't already heard, however.

"This isn't my first baby. I've had two more of 'em," she continued. "Real labors of love, they were. I didn't keep 'em long though— just gave 'em away, 'cause sooner or later the state will take 'em away from me anyway. I'm an unfit mother. I know it and the state knows it. I don't know why I feel different from most other women. I just do. I have no need to raise kids. All I've ever wanted to do was just party and have a good time. Well, I'm havin' it, ain't I?" Jolene asked, daring me to differ.

"Chasin' around and not stayin' in any one place for too long is what I do, and I'm not goin' to apologize for it!" Jolene said defiantly. I was becoming increasingly repulsed, even somewhat angered, by her attitude, especially regarding her children, but I tried to remain calm. "Jolene, it's up to you how you live your life, but you don't have to go through the inconvenience and problems of pregnancy if you don't want to. There are ways to prevent becoming pregnant." I didn't want to sound "preachy," but I wanted her to think about preventing future pregnancies.

"Yeah, I know all that, but I don't have the ways or means with me when I need 'em," she said in a singsong, mocking manner, adding cynically, "The kids are better off not knowin' who their dads are anyway. None of 'em are much good. Fact is, I'm not really sure I know who the real dads are, 'cept for this one. This baby's a 'love child.' This kid's dad told me he loved me the night we were gettin' it on. It wasn't just a grope in the dark this time. What ya lookin' at me for—don't you believe me?" Jolene asked defensively, waiting for some reaction from me that never came.

"I came to this shelter 'cause they can help me with the delivery of the baby, and the workers will do paperwork for the givin' away. I think my first baby probably died after I left the hospital. Talk was that it might. I never stuck around long enough to see what happened. It was small ... only weighed 'bout three pounds. I guess it was small on account of the alcohol I drank while packin' it. The second baby weighed four pounds; same reason. I don't know where that kid is now. A while back one place told me they'd give me an apartment to live in from the government, but I'd have to keep the kid. I told 'em no. I didn't much like the apartment anyway," Jolene said.

I exclaimed, "Jolene, you mean you had a chance to get government housing and refused it? Please reconsider this help, it may be your last chance to make things better for yourself," I warned, pleading with her to change her mind. She became belligerent and insulting. I ignored her insults.

Jolene was absolutely not interested in keeping her child, believing that was too big a price to pay for housing. She showed no sign of remorse or regret for any of her decisions. There wasn't a hint of concern or caring in her voice as she had spoken of the children to whom she had given birth. I was very disappointed in her decision to turn down government housing, though; it would have been a start in getting her life back on track. She went on, constantly voicing her own disappointments, complaining—whining, I suppose I now considered it—about her lack of this and her lack of that, moaning about her general well-being, the injustices in her life, her bad breaks, attacks on her person, slights from others, and more.

Finally, her litany of complaints ended and there were a few minutes of silence before Jolene spoke again. "I've struggled on the streets for years, 'cause that's all I know how to do. I haven't got any education other than grade school, 'cause my folks were poor and didn't have much learnin' either. I left home when I got my first promise of love. 'I'll take ya down to Disney World in Florida tomorrow or the next day, or anyplace else you wanna go after that,' Bobby Joe promised me. Sounded like heaven to me, so we just up and left right then and there. I left my share of the chores for someone else to do. Never even said goodbye to my own kin, just yelled 'goodbye holler, hello world' and left!

"I don't suppose I'll ever see a diploma with my name on it, but I'll bet ya I've had a lot of things happen to me only livin' my kind of life can teach a person. Sometimes I look in other folk's eyes and can see they don't think I'm worth much. I guess that's 'cause I mostly just party and drink the drinks men buy me for my favors," she said.

"I once had a frog named Bud—named him after the beer frogs. He died too soon. I used to feed him beer 'cause I figured he'd like it, too," Jolene solemnly stated. "Are you putting me on, Jolene?" I asked her. "No, ma'am, I'm tellin' ya the truth!" she said, and scolded me for not believing her.

There was silence for a few moments, then Jolene spoke again. "I'm not a prostitute though, 'cause nobody gives me any money for it; but I've done it for a case of beer, some pretzels, a roof over my head for the night, and a book of matches. 'Baby, won't ya light my fire?' Jolene sang, and then grinned. Going on, she said, "Guess I might be called a lotta other terrible names, though. Don't let this talk bother ya … this is the real world. Ya want my story, right?"

"Right," I replied. I suppose I should once again remind the reader that I've elided most of the profanity from our conversation, although I have presented what is quite possibly more unpleasant to many: Jolene's basic attitude. She continued, again revealing that she too dreamed of escaping her lifestyle—although by means of rescue by others, not effort on her part.

"I've sorta tried to get outa this kind of life, but never met a decent guy that I know of. I was with a guy once who was rich, though. Some people might think he's decent 'cause he's rich, but he wasn't. Some other dude pretended he was with me for a while, and then real sneaky-like he took me over to the 'fancy Dan.' My girlfriend knew who the rich guy was and told me he had a great big house and some kind of big business. She knew where his house was, so I asked her to drive me there. All I know is his last name. I saw it on his mailbox. It fits him too;… it was Leaver. I thought maybe he would come back to that bar and find me again, but he didn't. Maybe I was too easy to get, if ya know what I mean. Maybe it's 'cause I couldn't play the games he wanted me to play. 'You got something real pretty to dress up in?' he asked me. 'All I've got are these here clothes on my back. If ya want me to dress up in somethin' pretty, you're goin' to have to buy it for me,' I told him. And that ended that … he sure was stingy. He liked a good time, though, and really strutted his stuff," Jolene said, perhaps still trying to figure out where she went wrong.

"I'm thirty-seven years old now, so maybe I won't ever amount to nothin'. One time when I was really young my pa told me I wouldn't amount to much, but I didn't believe him. What did he know about amountin'? He wasn't much. I've never gone back home. I think my life isn't normal like most other people's, but it seems normal to me.

"I've gone to alcoholic meetings after I was arrested for drinkin'. I've been arrested for fightin' too. The people in charge of shelters won't let me stay in 'em if they can smell party on my breath when I get there. They've tried to teach me different jobs and things, and I do cleanin' work once in a while, but just don't have it in me to change too much. Maybe if I could stay in one program and have lots of help and comfort, I could stay off booze and get some school trainin'. Maybe I could get a job then. It might be a good deal for me. I guess men would always think I was dumb though, and I'd be right back to believin' 'em again," Jolene explained, revealing some of her thoughts about rehabilitation and its difficulties for her.

Jolene was sweating profusely and lifted her T-shirt/smock over her stomach so she could cool off a little before continuing. "I don't have many clothes to wear, especially since the robbery at the river. A thrift shop gave me these maternity clothes, and I'll still keep wearin' 'em after the baby goes. Ya know, I don't have much of anything.

"I told ya about my frog, Bud. When he died, I kept him on my blanket for most of the whole day before puttin' him back in the water. That frog cared for me. I know he did. I didn't have a dog, or a cat, or a man to keep me company, so I kept the frog instead. A person wasn't my answer—a frog was. He was there by the river anyway, so I adopted him. I know dogs, cats, or men won't stay with me for long, 'cause I don't live in a house. Besides that, I don't have money to feed them, so why would they want to stay with me? Dogs and men, though, they're a lot alike. Ya have to feed 'em, pet 'em, treat 'em nice, and let 'em out a few times a day! Then maybe they'll be happy and stay with ya. Most of the beds I've stayed in just had men in 'em who smelled like beer and sweat. I just try not to think 'bout what I'm doin'. The fact is, I'm pretty darn good at not thinkin' 'bout it," she said, revealing what I took to be her essential survival strategy. To think too much would seem to lead to unrelieved despair, since her frog story revealed that she, like virtually all humans, needed both to receive and extend love, however tough her outer shell and demeanor.

Jolene revealed more of her daily life. "If I'm travelin' about in town and can't make it back to the river, I usually sleep on park benches and beg for money from folks. If I have sex with some guy, that means I can usually stay with him all night and not have to sleep outside in the rain and cold. I've been chased out of a lot of places where I've tried to sleep before. 'Get the hell out of here or I'll call the cops!' they yell at me. I've heard it a million times.

"Some men have scared me half to death. One beat me up and left me in the woods one night, and for no reason at all that I could think of. I could feel my blood runnin' down my face, and could taste it, too. It was pourin' out my nose, and my lips were fat and kinda numb. I felt dizzy from being hit in the head, but remember the guy telling me, 'don't come outa the woods 'til mornin' cause I'll kill ya if I see ya stickin' yer head outa the trees. I'll be a watchin' for ya even tho' it's dark.' Well, he sure wasn't lyin' 'bout the dark. I couldn't see a thing! I was scared outa my wits, 'cause I knew there were wild animals in those woods. There'd been tales of how folks had been attacked by 'em. I talked myself into being calm. I sure didn't want that guy to find me again. I thought he was nuts! I hid in a pipe and put some weeds at one end of it 'til mornin' came. I didn't sleep one bit, and when it got light outside I looked all around for him, but he was nowhere to be seen," Jolene recounted.

"After not eatin' or drinkin' for more than a day, I thought a drink would taste pretty good. I found the main road and caught a ride back into town. I got drunk at the first bar I came to. Guys will always buy me drinks. I felt rotten inside and outside … a real 'no-good' feelin'. I was bloody and had cuts and bruises all over my body; but, as bad as I looked from the beatin' I took, the only thing the guys at the bar had to say to me was, 'Have a rough night, sweetheart?' Then they all laughed. A guy sittin' at the bar said, 'Yeah, she musta been workin' last night at the Women's Center for the Performin' Arts down by the river!' That nearly brought down the house! Another guy chimed in from one of the booths, 'I didn't know we had culture in this town. Where is this center?' The fella at the bar replied, 'The whorehouse down by the river!' Again, the whole place howled with laughter. I don't really wanna be from the dark, devil side of life like some of the people I've seen on 'Unsolved Mysteries.' I think most of 'em turn up dead," Jolene said, looking at me with a questioning look in her eyes. I think she was more worried than she let on to be about the dangers she faced.

Jolene then spoke softly, almost whispering, "Anyway, nothin' much matters to me anymore, 'cause nothin' is fun anymore. Sufferin' isn't much fun. Lonely isn't much fun, either. Maybe it's 'cause I'm just gettin' older now, but I feel like I should get a place to call my own. After the baby goes, maybe I'll feel different about stuff.

"If I only had some good friends to help me, maybe I could make some changes in my life. Maybe we could all talk about things that might help me out of this mess I'm in. I can't be thinkin' 'bout that now, 'cause I'm too sick. My life looks really dark right now. I feel low down and weak, and don't have much fight left in me. I don't get too excited about stuff either. If nobody gives me a baby shower, I don't care. What would be the sense of it? I'd just have to give the baby presents away with the baby anyway. I guess you're not havin' much of a good talk with me ... there's not much to write down that's good about me," she said, abruptly changing the subject. "I can't decide what to do or how to do it," Jolene said, somewhat sadly I believe, as she reached for a cold washcloth to put on her forehead. Did I correctly sense that maybe she would like a baby shower? It seemed that she knew she needed a more supportive group of friends, especially if she was going to rise above her situation. I believed I detected some cracks in her hard veneer.

Jolene glanced up at the clock on the opposite wall and said, "Damn, I need a drink bad! I can't quit my drinkin' or slow it down, either. If I have one drink, I just have to have another one, and then another, and before I know it, I'm drunk again. The guys are always makin' fun of me and callin' me names, and maybe they're right. Why am I worse than they are, though? Who buys me the drinks? They do, and they drink more than me. Somehow, they think it's different when they're wild and party. Once in a rehab class, our teacher told us that when we drink our brains don't get older to match our years, and part of our brains die, too, 'specially our 'right now or not too long ago memories.' Oh well, I don't have many good memories anyway, so what's the loss?" she said matter-of-factly. I suddenly thought of a maxim of la Rouchefoucauld that seemed appropriate: "Everyone complains of his memory, and no one complains of his judgements."

Jolene was candid about her condition and prospects for recovery. "The people at the detox places asked me how I could help myself stop drinking, and I told 'em that I would have to be locked up for a long time. Knowin' that scares me. Seems like I don't get back up so fast after the drinkin' anymore. My body aches more and I shake—look at me now! I'm startin' to shake again, ain't I? I don't feel good anymore. I'm startin' to wonder what will become of me. I've lived in places where I've been scared to death. Murders happen all around me on account of drugs and drinkin'. Those damn crackheads. They've ruined it for us alcoholics!" Jolene said, in a half-hearted joking manner, knowing the terrific toll that her lifestyle was exacting and its great risk to even her survival in the short term.

"I'm just so tired anymore that I can't watch out for myself. I need a watchdog at night. One of those pit bull kind. I don't have any family, and I don't wanna be around a lot of strangers. Maybe I'll start attendin' Alcoholics Anonymous when I get outa this shelter. I found out where one was by accident the other day when I was walkin' alone on the streets. I headed out past the Red Cross place and just kept on goin'. It's probably my only hope for makin' things better for myself," Jolene announced; but I wondered if she was telling me what she thought I wanted to hear? I never really knew.

Suddenly, Jolene asked me if I would help her up from her chair. "I've gotta get to the baby-check appointment. It won't be long now 'til I can leave here. I'm sorry if my story wasn't quite what you expected or wanted."

"Jolene, your story was just what I wanted," I remonstrated. "Stop selling yourself short;… and thank you for your song. You apparently don't realize what you have to offer the world." Cultivating her talent and having the discipline to manage it correctly, I'm convinced, could dramatically change her life for the better. "Jolene, maybe if you can end your dependency on alcohol, you can begin your singing career again," I said.

"Well, if I started singin' again, it would probably be in bars and I'd be tempted to drink. Maybe I'll just learn how to fly an airplane, or become a licensed hooker," she joked. "In that order?" I retorted.

Finishing our interview, I found myself voicing platitudes—all of which Jolene no doubt had heard before. She suddenly announced, "later lady," and slowly shuffled back up the hall and through the swinging door.

Kathleen

W ELL NOW, aren't you a good-looking cowboy!" I said to a young boy staying at a homeless shelter in Massachusetts. The boy promptly replied, "I'm pretending that I live on a ranch out in Wyoming and my Dad lives with us and rides horses with me."

"Do you go to school?" I asked him.

"No, I'm just a five-year-old and my momma home-teaches me here. We don't like the schools much anymore, 'cause the police checked the kids out at school and they had some bad drugs in their pockets. They're bad kids! My momma saw it and so did some other people," he replied, shrugging his shoulders. "I guess those fifth- and sixth-graders were just stupid kids who didn't say 'nope to dope.' They should've run away when the drug man showed up! I'd just get on my horse and ride off and go tell the sheriff that somebody was trying to kill me. I know how to call 911 all by myself, so if I couldn't find the sheriff, I'd just call that number. It's not much of a problem for me with those bad guys," he boasted. "I have to get up real early every morning 'cause this is the only stick horse here and there are lots of boys who need it," he said.

This little boy was undoubtedly one of the cutest, most animated children I'd ever met. His expressive brown eyes were framed with long, thick eyelashes. His complexion was olive and his hair was a shiny light-brown color. He was full of life and his enthusiasm was contagious. His voice was surprisingly low for such a young child, and he spoke quite loudly to make sure everyone heard what he had to say.

I was waiting in the main congregation area of the shelter for the executive director to find a woman interested in talking to me about her homelessness. Within ten minutes, a woman walked toward me, and, as she approached, she asked, "Is my little cowboy spinning yarns for you?" The young boy immediately stopped talking and waited for his mother to say something more. She introduced herself as Kathleen and her little cowboy as Brandon. She informed me that the director had asked her if she'd be interested in doing an interview about her homelessness and that she had consented, hoping to do her part to combat the problem.

Kathleen said, "Maybe if enough people informed others about the causes of homelessness it would become less common; but, as I've personally found out, it is impossible to avoid sometimes. Many of the people here at the shelter don't have good educations, and the less education they have, the lower their quality of life seems to be. That isn't the problem that brought my six children and me here, though," Kathleen said quickly, making sure I understood that her family wasn't to be mistaken for people who would make homelessness a way of life. She also made sure that her interview with me wouldn't be at the expense of her duties at the shelter, which consisted of cleaning the entire shelter, preparing the afternoon meal, and tending the pre-school children. My sister Lorine, who had accompanied me to the shelter, had graciously consented to take care of these duties for her so that our interview could be extended.

Kathleen was dressed casually, looking younger than her thirty-five years—probably because of her pretty baby face and ponytail hairdo. It seemed impossible that she was the mother of high-school-aged children. Somehow, her presence made a person feel that everything was going just fine. I enjoyed that. She looked around the big open room, with its cheerful walls filled with bookshelves and toys of all kinds. Brightly colored animals were painted across most of one wall, appearing as if they wanted to play too. Kathleen said, "Let's find a quiet corner and pull up a couple of comfortable chairs to sit on while we talk. I don't get a chance to relax very often. Surround me with luxury and comfort, world, anytime you want to," she joked.

Kathleen began our interview by immediately telling me that she had home-schooled all her children for the past three years. However, since coming to this shelter, she'd been forced to discontinue this practice and send them to public schools. Only two of her children did not attend public school—Brandon and his older brother John, a quieter version of the little cowboy. She related that problems arose for the family when their home burned to the ground. She told of the confusion and panic that went on as she made sure everyone had reached safety during the inferno. Brandon grabbed and hugged her leg very tightly, and she must have sensed it was time to reassure him that everything was going to be all right. She instinctively pulled him up on her lap and gave him a hug. "Be calm, be calm," Kathleen whispered, trying to allay her son's fears.

"The state has told me that when we live in a place of our own I can go back to home-schooling, and they'll provide help for me, if needed. My children have all been tested by the state to see if their education levels are equivalent to those of other children their age. I'm happy to tell you that they've all passed the tests given them. The state is satisfied at this point, and I'm proud of my efforts. I pulled my kids out of their public schools because I didn't like the way violence had escalated. There was so much trouble that metal detectors had to be installed at school entrance doors to increase safety.

"One morning as I was driving past my children's grade school, I glanced at the playground area and saw a drug bust being carried out by the local police department. I pulled my car over and walked to where a crowd was gathering just outside the fence. I gasped out loud as the police lined the children against the wall and searched them. It was like a scene from an action movie—hands up and legs spread! The police busted the grade schoolers for crack and cocaine possession. There it was. Right in front of me. Unreal! I hadn't heard about drugs until after I was out of high school. Probably the worst thing I could have done in grade school was to get caught with a box of candy cigarettes.

"The crowd watched in total disbelief. One grandpa of World War II vintage was mumbling to himself, becoming more angry by the second, and finally shouted, 'Our country could go down in a decade, just because the young people are all drugged-up and don't care about anything but their next fix. They won't be able to follow orders, or worse, they won't care about defending their country! That's what the drug supplying countries want and are counting on … our money, and to have control over the lives of our citizens. I guess the young kids think the "power rangers" will save them! What a joke!' And he stormed off. I had a sick feeling in my stomach as I watched what was going on, and I knew right then and there that I no longer wanted my children attending public schools. I immediately went into the school and withdrew them. I had just joined the ranks of the home schoolers," Kathleen announced.

"I feel very strongly about my children's safety and education, and I get upset when I think about all the traumatic events they have experienced at school: having their lunch money, clothes, and shoes stolen by force, threats of physical harm for one reason or another, and just plain being bullied by bad kids. I wondered how my kids could ever learn in such an environment. I hadn't wanted it to be like this, but it was. My young life was difficult and I was hoping to avoid hardships in the lives of my children. I usually don't talk much about my early childhood, but, in this case, I will," Kathleen said.

Her story jumped back in time to her own childhood, as she related, "Shortly after I was born my father left my mother. She raised me and most of my other brothers and sisters alone, until she finally remarried many years later. That union added seven more to our already large family. During my growing-up years, mother worked very hard just to get money enough for our food and shelter. She took care of elderly people in their homes. In fact, she helped them until the day before she passed away. She was amazing! Momma was a tiny woman, only five feet tall, but was strong for her size. Her patients' knew her strength and kindness, and so did her family. I never saw her rest her feet … not once.

"After graduating from high school, I entered a community college but had to drop out because I didn't have transportation during a bus strike in our area. I decided to find a job for a while and enrolled in a correspondence course so as not to waste my education time. My goal was to become a nurse, so I looked for a job in the medical field. I considered myself lucky after finding work at a local hospital. However, I soon had a major problem. A man working there was touching and pinching me every time I walked past him. He also whispered dirty words to me when I was within hearing range. I just couldn't put up with his unwanted sexual advances every time he got close to me. This type of behavior just leads to terrible consequences. I don't recall ever hearing the term 'sexual harassment' back then, but I knew his behavior was wrong and told my female supervisor what was going on. All she said to me was that it was 'all in fun and joking around.' Well, it wasn't fun, and he wasn't joking. I'd been terribly hurt by the consequences of a sexual experience earlier in my life. It happened at a time when I'd been too young to know how to handle the situation. I knew that I didn't want to endure any more pain than I already had in my life. I'm still living with the secret every day. I apparently didn't make a decision that I could live with.

"At any rate, I knew I couldn't tolerate this man's hushed voice, as he'd whisper his dreams and fantasies to me, not to mention the masculine endowments he claimed to possess. 'Oh, what a lucky, lucky girl you'll be if you'll just let me show you what a real man is like,' he'd brag. He made me sick! I was always watching out for him and never wanted to be alone with him if I could help it. I never once welcomed his advances. He was a lot older and seemed to hang around the very young, inexperienced girls who'd just been hired. The women in the office called him 'his royal fondleness.' He was definitely a predator.

"One morning as I approached the break room, I heard men laughing, and the man who was harassing me was boasting about how much I enjoyed his flirtations and advances. He said I was a 'hot little honey.' He was telling them lies about how far he'd gotten with me. I wanted to go in and claw his eyes out, but instead I went to my supervisor again and explained to her what I'd just heard in the break room. She was not at all sympathetic toward my show of innocence and complaining, and she again told me to tolerate the situation because 'this is just typical behavior for men.' She said, 'If you complain, they'll take some kind of retaliatory measure against you and make your work life miserable. This man is very valuable to our organization, so do the best you can with the situation.' I knew I was in an awful bind and wondered, 'How much more miserable can my work life be?' He was slandering my name, telling untruths about me, and causing me great anguish. I hated this situation even more, because I'd gone to a woman for help, not the typical male supervisor who'd held almost all of the supervisory positions in the workplace for the past century. Didn't she realize how her inaction was setting back any progress women had made toward sexual harassment?" (I'm sure Kathleen intended to say something like "ending sexual harassment," but I chose not to interrupt her train of thought by speaking.) "She could have resolved my problem and saved my job for me but instead chose to sacrifice my feelings, and my career, in favor of someone who was clearly violating my rights as a woman and as a human being. I'll never forgive this woman for turning her back, when she, as a woman, finally had the power to do something about this terrible abuse and chose to do nothing for her sister.

"After our meeting, I believed that I might be dismissed from my job without reasonable cause just to get rid of me for making waves. This would not look good on my record, so I went to the hospital personnel office and resigned. I cried all the way home. I was so tired from fighting battles of a sexual nature. I've always felt shame because of the vicious rumors this man spread. I'm sure that many of our co-workers believed his stories.

"I moped around the house for about a week before deciding that enough is enough! I went out and bought a newspaper and thumbed through the ads until I found a job at a nursing home. I figured the male hands there might be too old and tired to pinch me! Well, I was wrong again and was pinched at the home too! While working at the 'Shady Rust,' as it was affectionately called by the staff, I daydreamed constantly about getting a job somewhere else. Finally, a job was advertised for a position in the children's ward at a local hospital and I applied and was accepted. I'd always wanted to be a pediatric nurse and thought this was my big opportunity. I soon discovered that I just couldn't tolerate being around little children and see them suffer, or watch them being given away by their mothers so shortly after birth. I decided that perhaps the field of medicine was no longer the field for me, and quit this job, too."

She abruptly changed subjects, returning to what was obviously of great concern to her. "I've lived with my secret since I was a teenager. I know that it's taken a heavy toll on my personality and my relationship with others. I feel like my soul has been locked up and I'm not free to be the real me. There are a few people who know my secret, and I feel that every one of them owns a little piece of me. I should get counseling before there's nothing left of me," Kathleen said. I wondered if she would reveal the secret that was causing her such despair. She certainly seemed to need support and counsel from others concerning this matter, even though she feared exposing her deeper self.

She went on: "I was living with my sister in her apartment during this period in my life, and one day she asked me if I'd like to go out with a male friend of hers. She was probably tired of seeing me mope around, but I wasn't sure I wanted to meet anyone right then. I knew he lived in a town a great distance away and that we'd have to travel by bus for hours to get there. She kept asking and asking me to go, telling me that she knew I'd really like him, and that he was my perfect match. Finally, I agreed to go.

"We were to meet him at a dance. When we got there, I looked at my sister and asked, 'Which one is he?' She pointed to where he was sitting. Wow. He was worth the trip! I was immediately attracted to him, and there was an incredible feeling when his eyes met mine—nothing could have prepared me for the magic I felt. Suddenly, the dance hall turned into a ballroom for the new princess. I'd gone to a dimension somewhere over the rainbow. I didn't want to appear overly anxious, but the smile on my face probably gave me away. I thought he was exceptionally good-looking. He had shiny black hair that fell to the middle of his back, and his eyes were the most beautiful blue I'd ever seen. His eyelashes were so thick that I couldn't have counted them all in one lifetime. He had that 'lost little boy' look—what a sucker I am for that look! Yes, I'll admit to a total meltdown, but I didn't want him to know it. He dressed casually and carried himself well. He seemed self-assured and at peace with himself. His name was Louis. I found out that his family was French-Canadian from Montreal, but he was born in upstate New York.

"The next thing I knew he had stood up and was walking toward me. My heart stopped. 'Do you want to dance?' he asked me. I felt like he'd probably been coaxed to ask me, so I was uncomfortable. Did he really want to dance with me? Was it really his idea? I didn't know quite what to say to him, but finally said, 'Thank you for asking, but I don't think so. I've a feeling that dancing with me wasn't really your idea.' He assured me that he did want to dance with me, and hoped I'd change my mind and accept his invitation. I thought to myself, 'What have I got to lose? Besides, I'd driven a long way to meet him,' so I said 'yes,' and we've been dancing together ever since. My heart still skips a beat whenever he's around. Can you believe it?" Kathleen said, still smiling. "Of course, I've always thought our love was unlike all others," she added.

"Yes, I can believe it," I answered, though I knew she needed no reply from me.

"We eventually married and lived in Vermont for nearly ten years. Louis was a machinist and construction worker. When the housing industry fizzled, he lost his job. We stuck it out for a while and continued to look for work, but finally had to leave and look for work elsewhere.

"We traveled throughout most of the New England states looking for work, but came back and settled here in this part of Massachusetts.

Louis found work immediately and everything just came together. We had four thousand dollars left in savings when we moved here. We found our 'dream house' out in a wooded rural area, and had just completely furnished and decorated it when a fire burned it to the ground. We'd only lived there six months. We lost everything. Our landlord had told us he would get renters' insurance but hadn't done so before the fire started. We stayed with friends for a while and then moved to a motel until our money ran out. We were then forced to move into a shelter. The kids thought it was the end of the world. We took turns crying for weeks. It's like we'd lost our identify when everything burned, including the only pictures we had of our parents, our wedding pictures, school pictures, and important papers like birth certificates, baptismal certificates, diplomas, and scrapbooks. It seemed like we had no real identity any longer or proof of our lives."

She continued the sad recitation, although, as is the case with many accounts by homeless individuals, not all parts of it always seemed to make sense. Rather than interrupt with questions that could alienate those I was interviewing by seeming to doubt their accounts, I felt it best to let them tell their version of events, hoping I could unravel questions later. "Shortly after the fire, Louis's boss was sent overseas on business, and so we weren't getting paid. The company had to make some internal management and payroll arrangements so they could pay their employees. The next setback came when my husband had a few drinks and we were asked to leave the shelter. There are rules at all shelters that prohibit drinking. We relocated to this shelter, and the children and I have been living here ever since. Louis can't stay here because he drinks. He's the type of guy who, when the boss says, 'Let's stop for a couple of beers after work,' will say, 'Sure.' Well, he made the choice to do just that one night after getting off shift and was told to leave the shelter," Kathleen said, bringing their family's story to the present.

"We're trying to get enough money together to rent another place, and I'm trying to take care of the children so they'll have as little trauma as possible. It's a big job. Louis is putting money aside from each paycheck, and the children and I have some ideas and goals of our own," Kathleen said proudly.

Brandon began jostling around on his mother's lap and finally spoke up, "Our daddy is staying away from here because he drank some beer and got into trouble and can't come back. Momma, can I go have my afternoon treat?" Kathleen replied, "Yes, but clean up after yourself."

After Brandon had hopped down from his mother's lap, Kathleen said, "My husband is under a lot of pressure, too. When he's around, he does his part in trying to raise the children, and he disciplines them when they need it. Let's put it this way … there's a big difference in the kids' behavior when he's here and when I'm here alone with them. All he needs to do is give them a certain look and they mind. I can yell at them until I'm hoarse and don't get the same response. They look at me as if to say, 'Well, maybe we'll mind you, and maybe we won't!' Louis isn't allowed to come here between six and seven o'clock in the evening. That's the dinner hour. There are only certain times when he has visitation privileges. It's been too long a time since I've been able to say to him, 'Why don't you take a little time off work and come home early … before the kids get home.' I've always had a fondness for privacy. This is the longest Louis and I have been apart in eighteen years—it's been awful to endure. I love him very much."

Kathleen then shared her dream. "I have a plan for escaping our homelessness, and have had it for quite some time. My dream is to start up a business so my whole family can be together and work as a team. I submitted my application to a participating college for business counseling and testing to determine whether I was a good candidate for the Small Business Association [Administration] Women's and Minority Prequalification Loan Program. I passed the course, so there's a possibility of getting funding to help with our business plans. We want to operate a laundromat. Getting the capital is basically the only thing that stands in our way now. I've submitted an application and plans to the necessary agencies for assessment. I've found a potential location and we've completed a plan for start-up, including appliances and overhead. Of course, I'll use our family to operate the business.… I'm so excited! My daughters need to work, and so do my sons. We hope to all be together again, and, when we are, it will be so wonderful!

"Brandon and John helped me come up with some of the ideas for our business. We were staying at a motel and had just gotten back from a laundromat. The boys said, 'Momma, we have an idea. We can open our own laundromat, and we don't mean just a regular one. Those kinds are boring for kids. We can make a special one for kids.' The next thing I knew, everyone in our family added some ideas to the plan. The SBA says that I really can't add a bunch of gimmicks and changes until I get the original plan approved. The employees working at the approving agencies say that our plan will most likely be approved. Our idea is to one day have a place for children to play, with toys and games that will make them think for themselves and not have to be entertained by a machine or their parents. Also, we plan to serve food that both adults and children like to eat. Maybe within the next six months we can get started!" Kathleen exclaimed jubilantly.

A school bus returned the older children to the shelter. They were laughing and speaking at the same time, as they excitedly described the experiences of their day at school to their mother. It was evident they loved and respected her. Kathleen said, "It hasn't been easy adjusting to public schools, but the children seem to be doing fine except for an occasional accident. My eight-year-old boy fell and cracked his skull on the concrete while playing during recess. It took more than a year for the swelling to go down. One day while playing at the first shelter where we stayed, he was kicked in the head by one of the other boys staying there, resulting in a terrible seizure. This boy knew about my son's head injury, but kicked him anyway. Sometimes the shelters have unmanageable children staying in them, and parents have to watch constantly to protect their children from danger. I guess this is a problem no matter where a person lives," she added; but she had revealed to me an aspect of homelessness or living in a shelter that I had not really thought about before.

"I have two teenaged daughters," Kathleen continued. The oldest one is sixteen years old and won't be back at the shelter today because she's staying overnight at a friend's home. I always check on my children to make sure they're where they are supposed to be, and I insist on meeting the parents of their friends before I'll let them stay at their homes. My oldest girl is exceptionally pretty but is very shy. She doesn't think she's pretty, mostly because we're homeless. We've told her that many girls believe they are ugly when they're that age, and it doesn't matter if they are the most beautiful girls in school, they can still feel ugly. She doesn't want anyone at school to find out that she lives in a shelter, and has gone to great lengths to fool her classmates. The girls never host slumber parties here, of course. I simply must mention our school bus driver. She is one of the most thoughtful people in the world, and picks up the homeless shelter kids first and drops them off last. That way, the other students won't know where they live."

Kathleen leaned farther back in her chair and was quiet for several moments before continuing. "Our fourteen-year-old daughter is just the opposite. She thinks she's gorgeous! And she is. Recently, she was asked by one of the local modeling agencies to submit a picture portfolio. We didn't have the $189 dollars to do so, and the opportunity was lost. We believe it was divine intervention.

"The children have gone through moods of depression over being homeless, especially when we had to move to the second shelter. They felt helpless because they had no control over their homelessness, and asked us, 'Did we have to come all this way, just to stay in shelters?' The staff and counselors explained to them that it can happen to anyone. The staff here really like our kids, because they're not spoiled and always help with the cooking and cleaning and don't mind tending the little children. Amazingly, they seem intact emotionally, and I feel they'll be ready for most things in life as a result of their experiences here. They've learned how to survive and start from scratch to improve their lives. I still have a lot to teach them about the dangers they must avoid. The fight between good and evil has never been greater, and there will always be others who will try to tempt my children into doing destructive things. At each new school, another group of bad kids are there, eager to destroy my kids by offering them a welcome basket of drugs, sex, and other temptations that can send them to their private hell. Like the old saying, 'misery loves company.'

"Now that my kids aren't around, I'll tell you about *my* private hell. I lost my virginity when I was only fourteen years old. I let someone who was older talk me into having sex. What a terrible mistake that was for me to have made. I'll always pay for my error in judgment. I have seven children, not six. My oldest child, a little boy, was born when I was just fifteen years old. I raised him for more than two years before putting him up for adoption. I wasn't old enough to take care of him and provide for him. I've regretted my decision every day of my life since I gave him away. Of course, I was not married and never had the means nor the maturity to keep and raise him. I can't forget, though, no matter how hard I try. That is my secret.

"I knew nothing about sex when I became pregnant. I had to learn the hard way. My mother was very strict and sex was never discussed in our home. Since sex was a forbidden subject, I just didn't realize all the trouble I could get into. I never realized there was a 'big picture.' A young person definitely needs the love, support, and guidance from parents to learn the values necessary to make good choices in their life. I was young and ignorant about sexual things, but I promised myself that if I ever had daughters I'd definitely see that they had the knowledge, and not just a snippet of knowledge, to save themselves from the heartbreak I've had to endure," Kathleen confessed.

"My secret has truly been a terrible cross for me to bear all these years, and has put a damper on any happiness or success I've achieved in my life. I know I'll live with my pain until the day I die. Every day I wonder … what does my first son look like now, where is he living, is he still living, what is he doing, and is he happy? Does he wonder who his real mother is, what she looks like, and if she loves him? She surely does," a very sorrowful mother answered her own question. Kathleen has apparently kept her secret from her children. She never mentioned whether or not her husband knows about her having had a child during her teenage years.

"We'll go on here for the next few months, and if our prayers are answered we can begin again. In the meantime, we'll be the best family we can be," vowed a very determined woman, who closed our interview by saying, "We, as a family, need each other to be strong, though sometimes my hope flickers." I can only hope that it stays alive, for her story had kindled a greater hope in my own heart as I continued to try to understand more fully the plight of homeless women in America.

Colorado ▬▬▬▬▬▬▬▬▬▬▬

ONE AFTERNOON in July 1996 I arrived at a college town in Colorado. The day was beautiful but very hot. Exhausted from travel and sure that a heat stroke was imminent, I stopped at an ice cream shop, and, purely as a means of survival, ordered a Hawaiian yogurt fruit shake. As I savored each delectable mouthful, my energy level rose and I soon regained a general sense of well-being.

Across the street was a beautiful park, and I watched the children on the playground equipment showing off for their parents. I remembered how freely I had played as a child living in a rural area in Wisconsin. All the neighborhood children played from dawn till dusk— sliding down haystacks, playing the games of childhood, swinging from anything we could hang a rope from, riding horses, going to the park, swimming in ponds, or "just being" in the great outdoors. Mothers gave each child a sack lunch and told us to make sure we were home before dark. There are too few places on earth today where a child can enjoy this kind of freedom and play with such abandon.

I watched a beautiful young mother as she wearily pushed a baby stroller on the sidewalk in front of my car. A small blanket was draped across the bonnet of the stroller to keep the sun out of the baby's eyes. A boy about six years old was walking alongside his mother. He appeared to be very tired, stumbling every few steps. A little girl, just slightly smaller than the boy, was walking behind everyone else, dragging an enormous doll by the hair. The children's cheeks were red from too much sun and their hair was damp from sweat. The small group continued up the sidewalk, then waited at the corner for the traffic light to change so they could cross to the park.

117

A large, old tree served as an umbrella for the tired travelers, and they settled down on the cool green grass. It all looked so inviting that I decided to go over and enjoy a shady area next to them. I sat with my back up against a giant old tree, watching and contemplating. I thought about days gone by when I'd taken my children and grandchildren to parks and watched them play. The young mother saw that her children were comfortable. She took the blanket off the carriage and placed it on the ground to sit upon. The little girl said, "Momma, tell us a story you haven't told us before. You can even make it up if you want to." The mother began speaking in a soft voice, telling her children about their surroundings and about good manners; she also encouraged them to be inquisitive about things. Her long silky hair was a warm brown color, and she had fine delicate features. She wore a long skirt with a muted batik pattern in autumn colors; her blouse was ivory. A silver cross adorned her neck, next to her sleeping baby's face. She and her little ones presented a charming picture, and I hoped it would presage a good day for me.

I had journeyed hundreds of miles to speak with homeless women in this city and would soon be stopping at the missions, shelters, emergency services, soup kitchens, and other places where homeless people gathered. The first place I look for information about finding homeless women is in the yellow pages of a local telephone book. I usually find what I need to know under headings like Shelters, Homeless, Women, and Social Services, as well as through church listings of all denominations.

Women who need emergency assistance can also use this method for finding help. Hopefully, they will have the money for a phone call. If not, there are agencies and churches who allow individuals to use their telephones. Probably the best option for the homeless is to go to the nearest church; many are open night or day. Good people at the churches help in so many ways, and there is no red tape. Employees working at the resources listed in the telephone book usually have printed handouts listing names, addresses, and telephone numbers for all available services in the city. These printed handouts give current information about such things as social service offices, church programs, shelters, food kitchens, clothing centers, jobs, educational workshops, medical and dental assistance, and child care.

After leaving the park, I soon found a phone booth. I reviewed information on available services in the city and decided to call a mission operated by the Catholic church. I asked those in charge if I might speak to some of the homeless women staying there. The clergyman was most helpful and told me, "the mission will be open this evening after seven o'clock, and the evening meal will be ready to serve shortly thereafter. The women will be staying overnight and will leave before seven o'clock in the morning. They'll be on the streets all day long during the summer months. If you wish to speak with any of them, it will have to be after their evening meal."

I drove to the secluded, peaceful mission on the outskirts of the city and introduced myself to the staff, which consisted of postgraduate students with degrees in sociology and a member of the clergy. They helped the homeless with their immediate shelter and personal needs, fed them, and provided educational and job-related assistance and counseling. One important service I noticed immediately: hugs from the staff to all who entered the shelter. The clergyman in charge of the mission spoke quietly and appeared to be a very kind and humble man. I felt at peace, simply because of his presence, his mannerisms, and his words. He led gently. This mission was truly a sanctuary where the homeless could find safety and refuge. It followed Saint Paul's counsel: "Always be joyful, pray constantly; and for all things give thanks."

I arrived early, before the evening meal was ready to be served. Homeless women were sitting under some large trees on the beautiful grounds of the mission. I introduced myself and asked, "Do you mind if I sit and talk with you about your homelessness and how you are doing here at the mission? I promise not to keep you from your evening meal." I began our conversation by telling the women about my visits with other homeless women across the United States and how they were dealing with the problems they faced.

The women introduced themselves. Pat and Roberta were sitting next to each other and told me they were from North Carolina. After arriving in town, someone had told them about this Catholic mission. They came and stayed while gathering their energies and making plans to begin again. Their words related how very grateful they were to have been able to stay at the mission during their transition period. A woman named Elaine said she was from Nebraska and joined in the conversation. She pointed toward her children playing tag around the big trees, and said, "I'm so happy to hear the laughter of my children again. I can withstand many things, but I cannot bear to see my children hungry or unhappy."

The husbands of Pat and Roberta had lost their jobs when the plant where they worked in North Carolina relocated out of the country. They could find no other work in their hometown or close by, so the decision was made to leave. Saying goodbye to friends and relatives and leaving their homes had been a heartwrenching experience for these women, and having to uproot their children from their schools, churches, friends, cousins, and grandparents was even more difficult. It was traumatic for some of the children, and their fears were manifested by acts of bedwetting, not wanting to eat, crying, and silence, among other things. Some families from the plant were moving to Arkansas to work in the chicken industry, but these people had no desire to do that. They heard that Colorado was experiencing tremendous growth and that the construction industry was booming. This news sounded encouraging, so the families decided to head farther west for a better life.

The families traveled in an appropriately named Voyager van, towing a trailer that held their possessions. With 155,000 miles showing on the odometer, it was not too surprising when the van had engine trouble in Arkansas. The men walked about five miles before finding help. When they returned to the van with parts to repair the problem, they found that one of the children was in terrible pain and appendicitis was suspected. The family and the ill child returned to town with the man who'd given the men a ride. Their fears were confirmed by physicians and immediate surgery was performed. The little girl was released from the hospital within a week, while the travelers stayed at the home of a nearby minister during the unexpected ordeal. The operation and other expenses wiped out what little money Pat's family had saved to begin their new life, but they were happy that the money had been there to help their child. The travelers faced challenges but never quit. After arriving in Colorado, the families needed compassionate help, which they found at the Catholic mission.

Roberta told me, "Both our husbands are working now and are happy with their jobs. We women have part-time jobs and work opposite shifts so we can exchange babysitting chores to help each other. It won't be long now until we can afford a big old house and all live together and get off the streets. Eventually, we'll branch out and begin our lives again." I noticed that the adults talked bravely especially when the children were around. Despite being down on their luck they were good, sturdy, godfearing people—actually Protestants, in fact—and had a lot of faith. I felt fortunate to have met them and pleased at the help that a Catholic organization extended to less-fortunate members of other faiths. My day was becoming better and better.

An attractive black woman introduced herself as Dolly, and showed a set of deep dimples when she smiled at everyone. She was friendly— one of those people you just love to be around, the type you almost hang on their leg to keep them from leaving. She told us, "Today is my sixty-first birthday, girls, just one year away from my Social Security check, but I have no one to celebrate my birthday with! I'm all alone and single, an unclaimed treasure is all. Someone will have a good companion if they'll just connect with me and give me a fair shake. Sure, I have old memories—some good, some bad, but they're not heavy baggage; they don't weigh my butt down! I just think about them once in a while. Living in an alley in Newark, New Jersey, was not where I wanted to live out my golden years, so I hitched a ride to Denver with a trucker. He thought I was kidding at first, but I convinced him that I was serious about needing a ride. I told him that I had a friend in Denver. He joked, 'I hope I don't get pulled over for transporting a senior citizen across state lines!'

"Leaving Jersey was sad. I'd lived there my entire life. But, at the end of my stay there, my vocabulary was down to just three words— 'leave me alone!' It was too hard and dangerous to continue living on the streets, because I was getting on in years. My bones ached from sleeping on hard benches, cement sidewalks, and the ground. To make a long story short, when I got to Denver, I found out that my friend had died. I've been on the move ever since, but maybe I'll stay here in Colorado. I'm hoping that I'll find a life for myself before winter."

Every woman in the group took a turn giving this lovely lady a hug and a hearty "Happy Birthday, girl!" A woman who had left a town where she'd lived her entire life, set out to find a new life at sixty years of age, dared travel across country with a total stranger, lost her one friend to the grim reaper, and could still laugh at it all had to be one strong woman!

Sitting on the lawn with these new friends was a bit akin to being a teenager at a slumber party. We were all having a good time telling our stories, using such prefaces as, "well that's nothing," "well, top this," "you won't believe what happened to me," "you're putting us on," "no way," and others. I then happened to glance up from the circle of ladies in time to see the woman I'd seen at the park earlier in the day. I gasped—she was a homeless woman—and had walked about three miles from town to get here, not to mention all the walking she'd done during the day. I'd had no idea what her circumstances were when I first saw her. If only I'd known, I could have given her a ride to the mission. It was almost heartbreaking now to see her and those tired little children. They slowly approached the mission entrance. Several hours had passed since I'd last seen those tired, red-faced little children and their weary mother. As she pushed the stroller toward the door of the mission, I could hear the children whimpering. The mother was exhausted, and bowed her head as she passed us. The clergyman must have seen them coming too, because he held the large doors open so the little group could enter. I thanked God for these shepherds who had a place for the little family to stay.

The bells tolled, and a slight breeze escorted everyone into the mission for the evening meal. The clergyman asked me, "Would you like to join us in celebration of the dinner hour and eat with us?" I declined, and explained to him that I'd eaten just before arriving but was extremely honored to have been invited. I continued, "The bench under the trellis looks inviting, so I'll just sit there and wait for the ladies to finish their meal, if that's okay with you. Also, I have a favor to ask of you and feel very humble in asking. If you have a chance to speak to the little mother who just pushed the stroller into the mission, would you please ask her if she'd be interested in granting me an interview? I know her and the children are extremely tired tonight, so if she's too tired for an interview tonight maybe she'll consent to one in the morning. I'd be happy to take her and her little family to the park or anywhere else she wants to go." The priest replied, "Yes, the sweet Spanish lady and her children. I'll see what I can do."

I walked to the bench and sat down, removing my camera from the leather backpack I held on my lap. The battery was still good and there was enough film for pictures. I also checked my tape recorder to make sure the batteries were working and there was enough tape for an interview. I seemed to be prepared. I'd been sitting for several minutes, not paying attention to the outside world, when suddenly I realized a man smelling of alcohol was in front of me. He yelled, "What the hell are you doing here at the mission? What do you want with us?" He screamed loudly and the veins stuck out in his neck.

I instinctively took a deep breath and replied, "I'm here to interview the homeless women staying at the mission." He poked me in the throat with a long-nailed finger and screamed, "What's in it for you?" I answered, fearfully, "I'm writing a book about the lives of homeless women." He screamed again, "You don't give a damn about these women, and I aim to drive you out of here so you won't bother them!"

Before I could say another word, he yelled loudly, "Do you know what a buck is?" I cautiously replied, "There are different kinds of bucks. Are you talking about a dollar?" He shook his head back and forth and shouted, "You dumb bitch. I'm not talking about a dollar!" I asked, "Are you talking about a male deer?" He displayed real rage and yelled, "Oh, give it up lady! I am the only 'buck' you need to know about. I'm a Cajun buck and the storm is ragin'! I don't need society; belonging is impossible because of what society did to us years ago. All I have now is pain, shame, and guilt because of the *fine* citizens of this country. Do you understand what I'm saying? Do you like my mask? You don't see the real me! We don't need any more of what this country dishes out, and that includes you, you little do-gooder bitch! My heart doesn't beat with good feelings anymore. Those feelings have been beaten out of me because of the deeds the wonderful people in power have made me do. Those bastards! I don't want to be a part of that place anymore, but I can't escape it. Do you understand me?" he ranted, shoving me farther back on the bench and awaiting a reaction from me.

I knew I basically was trapped but tried not to panic. Unfortunately, I couldn't see anyone else outside the mission. He grabbed my camera and threw it at me, hitting my outstretched hands that I was using for protection. "You want to take a picture of a homeless person? Well, take my picture! No? I'm not good enough? Go ahead and spit at me, others have! Do it now! I protected you with my life and you betrayed me, deserted me, and abandoned me! I trust only myself. Do I look like a man who's afraid because of what I've done and where I've been? Don't you look at me like I'm crazy! Are you going to ask me to tell my story? Are you going to ask society to help me? Are you my salvation, you bitch? Are you afraid of me? Do you think I'm not worth saving? Or am I just a 'nothing' who is disappearing more and more every day? Hey lady, are you going to help me?" he asked, as he ended his tirade of questions.

I started speaking slowly and quietly. I knew my voice was trembling, but I also knew that I had to protect myself, so I continued, "I believe I understand what you're trying to tell me. I'll venture a guess that you were a soldier in Vietnam. There are programs to help you regain some of what you've lost." I expressed my sympathy and shame at the injustices and pain Vietnam War soldiers endured. I told him that I had been to the monument in Washington, D.C., and was overcome as I looked at the names of the men who lost their lives. When I talked of the bravery and courage it takes to go into battle, he mocked me as a weak woman who didn't know what she was talking about.

I told him that I saw tokens of remembrance—pictures, letters, poems, small American flags, and flowers placed in front of the wall. I saw a long-stemmed white rose and a message of love written on paper and placed in a pair of polished combat boots. I saw the model of a small red Corvette that surely must have resembled the one waiting back home for a soldier. I wept unashamedly at that wall. I told him that I was not the one to help him but that he shouldn't discourage me from trying to help women in the country who are homeless. I told him that he needed to get in touch with the Department of Veterans Affairs and give them another chance to help him. "You hate the government, the political leaders, and anyone else in authority who wronged you. Maybe you're right. I don't know. I do know you soldiers followed the rules of war and the orders you were given. I know all that, and believe me, I'm grateful for your sacrifices and so are millions of other Americans. We are proud of you," I told him.

I finally decided to look up at this man who frightened me. I had listened to him. I had responded. I was too shocked by the whole experience to say any more. He stared at me with a hateful look. His stance was wide and his arms were folded. His posture was one of control and aggression. "Give me a reason," he said in a combative tone.

Suddenly I heard the most beautiful voice calling out, "The women have finished their meal. Would you like to come in?" It was the priest. After quickly gathering my equipment from the ground and stuffing it into my pack, I stood and walked rapidly toward the mission entrance. The angry, troubled veteran remained standing. After a few minutes, I looked out the window and saw him sitting on the bench, leaning over with his head in his hands.

I told the staff what had happened outside. I explained to them that I was still upset and would prefer to leave and come back in the morning to interview one of the homeless women. A member of the staff reminded me that the women would be out on the streets again in the morning after seven o'clock. She told me that I might run into some of them at a job search site, a soup kitchen, or a park, and gave me addresses of those places. I asked the priest to please walk me to my vehicle, past the man on the bench.

Early the next morning I searched all over town for the homeless woman and her three little children, but saw only the troubled veteran. One of my deep regrets will always be not being able to find the beautiful Spanish lady. It is my hope that the veteran will find the help and peace he so desperately needs and deserves and that the homeless woman and her children will also find a home. The veteran defended our homes and homeland, yet now he has no home; and the homeless woman must defend herself and her children without the safety of a home. I think this story should be told, even though the interview didn't go as I had planned. Events such as these happen daily in the world of the homeless.

Starr ══════════════════════

THE ACTRESS Whoopi Goldberg has a look-alike. I have called her Starr, and she's a homeless woman dividing her time between the beaches and streets of Delaware and Maryland. The two women share similar facial features, especially the wonderful smile, and both seem to possess outgoing, fun-loving personalities. I met Starr at The Bend in the Road, a daytime refuge for homeless women. She had just used the shower there, dressed, and was ready to begin her day. I'd spoken to the director of the center earlier, and had been told that Starr would be a good woman to interview. I was happy when I learned that she had agreed to speak with me about her homelessness.

Many homeless women remain in a rather dishevelled state—unwashed hair, faces, and clothing—but not Starr. When we met, she was wearing white jeans and a T-shirt. Her hair was styled in braided corn rows, with colorful beads securing the end of each braid. She ushered me into an upstairs office at the center, where she took care of a few important duties before beginning our interview. After listening and watching her for several minutes, it was evident to me that Starr was bright and energetic. She interacted well with the other female tenants and with the administrators at the day center. Her ideas were workable and her enthusiasm was contagious.

"Here we go! My interview will be both frank and honest," Starr said, after completing a phone call. She began, "I guess you can call my story, 'Married in Dover, Didn't Think it Over!' Is that all right with you?" she laughingly asked. "I met my guy, Willie, in Dover, Delaware. We were both musicians having a good time playing in a band. We lived together for five years and had a four-year-old daughter we named

Melody. One day we just decided it was probably a good idea to get married. That's when our troubles started. My Willie thought the 'I do' part of the wedding ceremony meant, 'I do wanna go back home and live with my momma!' So, after the ceremony, the three of us immediately moved in with his mother. Can you beat that?"

"Well," I replied, "we Norwegian brides had some strange concerns in the 1800s. Seems a bride was thought to be vulnerable to the magic of evil beings, and was guarded and protected. There were old tales about brides being abducted by trolls and netherworld beings. The door of the wedding reception hall was slammed three times to scare away evil beings. Gunshots were fired over the bride's head and over the wedding procession on its way to church. And the shooters most likely had been drinking!"

"I don't know which tale is the worst," Starr said, "but after I'd lived with Willie's momma for a week or two, I didn't think anything could have been worse. I noticed that Willie was slowly but surely starting to slack up on some of his responsibilities. He seemed to be going backward in age and not acting as grown up as he had when we'd first met. Willy seemed to have decided that he didn't want to be a grown-up man any longer. He now wanted to let the women in the house take care of him."

The phone rang and Starr answered it, informing a homeless woman about the services provided at the shelter. When her call was finished, she continued her story. "Well, honey, about my growing awareness that Willie was acting more and more like a momma's boy … that was then and this is now, and it's now my turn to call a few of the shots in my life. I won't settle for anything less, either." She imparted some advice to readers of the book: "Wake up, mommas, and kick those big boys out and make them grow up! You're not breaking the chains that will free them up to be responsible men. I don't understand the sisters putting up with these mommas' babies. If a sister sees this going on, she better flat-out run! Those big boys aren't going anywhere. They're losers and you'll be a loser too if you stay with them."

She continued her story. "My feelings were strong that Willie would continue his role as a momma's baby, but I also knew that he had a brother and sisters his momma had taught to move out of the house. I was trying to get him to move out too, but hope was running out. I finally said, 'We're married now. Your momma doesn't want you to live in her house anymore.' He said, 'She does too!' He just hesitated and hesitated, did nothing, and got drunk! Not my idea of a swift, decisive move. Then I started thinking that maybe momma had decided she didn't like living alone. I couldn't read their minds … or could I? Maybe they'd made a pact to drive me out," Starr said, confessing that she had not fully understood the actions of her husband and mother-in-law.

"I soon found out that momma was abusive too. One day shortly after Willie and I moved in with her, she picked up a baseball bat for no apparent reason and chased me around the house. As she chased me, Willie was yelling for me to 'hide here, hide there!' Can you just picture this going on with a bunch of adults? 'Stop her! Stop her!' I screamed at him. 'Oh, that's just my momma,' he'd yell back. She was screaming at me the whole time she was chasing me! The woman was nuts!"

"What was she yelling?" I asked Starr. "Something about career opportunities in Haiti, maybe," she said, and then more seriously responded, "Oh, something about me trying to give orders around her house when it wasn't my place to do so. Willie must have confided in her about my wanting him to move out on our own."

Starr was tickled with her thoughts and suddenly burst into laughter, "Enough time has gone by now that I can make jokes about this period in my life. I tell people that I've seen rabid dogs with less foam on their mouths than my mother-in-law had on hers, and she never wore a leash! Another funny story I tell about her is the time she threw one of her house plants at me and a gopher jumped out of it! I tell people that's when I knew she was a loser for sure."

Starr continued her story, "You've got to understand, honey. She didn't like me right from the start and made no bones about it. I tried to figure out why—maybe everything hadn't been on her terms and her position as drill instructor was threatened. Whatever the reason, I felt like I was definitely an outsider, and I was very uncomfortable with the living arrangement. One day after having endured the wrath of momma for two months, I told her how I really felt about her constant criticism and crazy fits. The next words out of her mouth were, 'Get outa my house!' I guess momma was downsizing.

"When Willie came home from work that evening, I told him what had happened, and he simply said, 'I like living with my momma and plan to continue living with her.' I was stunned! Willie then told me he wasn't going anywhere with me. I couldn't believe it. My heart pounded.

I thought we had a deeper relationship, but apparently I was wrong. Willie seemed to have the spine of a melting candle.

"My daughter and I left the house as soon as I packed our things," she recalled. "I really had no choice in the matter. It wasn't my house and I'd been told to leave. Simple as that. As the front door 'hit me in the ass,' as Willie had so eloquently phrased it, I heard a small voice quietly saying, 'Goodbye, daddy.' It was Melody's voice. In my mindless stupor I'd forgotten about her and what she must be feeling and thinking. I never really listened to the endless questions she asked me as we walked to a telephone booth about ten blocks from the house. To this day, I don't recall my answers or the reasons I gave her about why we were leaving and where we were going. I felt small, like a fish being thrown back into the lake by a fisherman because of its size. I was in a state of panic and had a worthless, foolish feeling as I thumbed through the torn pages of the phone book. In fact, I felt like the torn and wrinkled pages, too."

She looked for the telephone number of a homeless shelter where they could spend the night, not knowing what else to do. "I hoped we could stay at a shelter long enough to get on our feet. I only had four quarters and a five-dollar bill in my pocket.… My farewell scene with Willie kept playing over and over in my head as I tried to function normally and find a number for a shelter," Starr related. "I remembered him saying to me, 'You came into this house with no money and you'll be leaving the same way you came.' I'd worked outside our home nearly every day since I'd met him. What was he talking about? I was numb and unbelievably saddened after finding out that Willie wasn't going to leave with me. I only vaguely remembered stumbling around the bedroom as I slowly picked up our belongings. I was too surprised and hurt by the sudden turn of events to feel any hate toward Willie— yet. I guess you could say I was in shock.

"With my third quarter, I found the number of a shelter where we could stay. The bad news was that the shelter was across town." They took a bus, she remembered, stating, "After we were seated, I just knew everyone aboard had figured out we were homeless. Melody soon fell asleep on my lap, exhausted from the events of the day. Tears streamed down my face as I realized what a mess we were in. When we arrived at the shelter, a kind-looking woman greeted us with a firm handshake. I knew we'd be safe for at least the night. I hoped she could help me with our new beginning but decided to worry about our future in the morning," Starr said, detailing the events that had left her almost crazy with anxiety and introduced her to the streets.

Starr said she recounted her day and tried to assess her situation after Melody was in bed. "My homelessness really surprised me. How had it happened? Why didn't Willie want to live with us or help us? Didn't he love us? Hadn't he ever loved us? Was it his alcohol that made him incapable of honest feelings and the ability to love and reason? Did his mother influence his decision? I had so many unanswered questions whirling in my head that first night, and I was awake for several hours before finally falling asleep.

"Willie had always worked as an electrician during the day, and in the evenings he played in a band that included me and three other musicians. He was at least a semifunctioning alcoholic. We could have bought our own place if Willie had gotten his act together. He knew I hadn't been the reason his mother was so downright mean. It wasn't fair to me and Melody to have to leave this way," she maintained, obviously concerned that I understood the beginnings of her homelessness.

Starr spoke about the origin of her relationship and her brief marriage to Willie, claiming that at the time she met and became involved with him she hadn't realized he was a heavy drinker. "Then I moved in with him and began to smell liquor on his breath when he came home from work each night. After cleaning up each evening after work, we had dinner and then would go directly to the clubs and play with the band. We were good together at the beginning of the evening, but the more Willie drank, the more out of control he became. He started getting bossy with me and then bossy would turn into mean. Alcohol ruined his personality. I'd get so nervous! I also learned that he'd been married before and his former wife had been a drug addict. They had a son, and I learned that his son had found his mother dead, with the needle still stuck in her body after she'd overdosed. They lived in California at the time of her death. I should've been smarter about what I was getting into before we got pregnant. I'd seen a few of the problems Willie had, but ignored them. We married in September and his momma kicked me out in November. So much for the 'till death do us part' I'd heard at our wedding ceremony.

"After a few days of crying at the shelter, one of the supervisors suggested that as soon as I felt a little stronger I go to the Division of Social Services and obtain help and legal aid and let them assist me in putting my life back together. She told me that the workers there could instruct me about how to get a divorce, if that was my desired course of action. So, early one morning, Melody and I went to the agencies dealing with our kind of problem. I filled out the paperwork they gave me, but when it was checked by the clerk she told me that a divorce wasn't possible for at least two years. She also told me that there would probably be no support from the state for us. It was hard for me to believe this was true. The clerk said, 'You're young, healthy,' and this, that, and the other. 'You can't get any help through Social Services because you're married and your husband makes good money.' Trouble was, he wouldn't give me any of it. So, I wasn't getting any help from Willie, and divorcing him meant hiring a lawyer and going to court, and I couldn't do that without money. I couldn't get help from the agencies until I was divorced or Willie declared his income through them. Willie would not respond to my telephone calls. Was this limbo? With no money, I was dead in the water. In fact, we've never gotten a divorce. I couldn't pay for one. He didn't want one. To this day I'm still married to him. I can't believe it," Starr said.

I wondered why she hadn't been more aggressive in forcing her husband to pay child support through the court system, and she told me that she felt she wasn't worth much and didn't want to set herself up for rejection again.

"Day after day I called Willie and left messages with his mother for him to call us, but he never bothered. Maybe she never even gave him the messages. I don't know. One evening I phoned and found him at home. I was both relieved and apprehensive at the same time. After all, I hadn't spoken to him since I'd left his momma's house. I asked him if he wanted to see me and discuss how we were going to take care of our daughter. I told him that we'd been living from shelter to shelter, as each had rules as to how long we could stay. He just yelled, 'you left!' and then hung up on me. I was stunned. I waited for more than a year but never heard from him again. I became very bitter and decided never to trust a man again. I finally decided to call my mother in Detroit and let her know about the trouble I'd been in for the past year. I also asked her if I could come back home and bring Melody with me. I felt better after making some kind of decision. I'd given up hope that my husband wanted us. It had been a hard year since our parting.

"The next morning I took my little girl's hand and headed for Traveler's Aid to see if they would give us money for the bus trip home to Detroit. I didn't want Melody to have to continue the refugee bit any longer. The streets were dangerous. I also didn't want her to hear that she was 'poor welfare trash' ever again. She would be safe with my mother and family and could play with her cousins, have her own room, and wake up in the same bed every morning. A few people were lined up waiting to be helped at the aid station. I prayed there would be money enough when it was our turn for help. I felt very fortunate when we got the fare and boarded the bus. My mother had told me that we could both live with her until I was in a position to afford a place to live. When she picked us up at the bus station my little daughter cried and said, 'Grandma, it was so awful living in the shelters. I was so scared and some people made fun of me.' It felt good to be with family again," Starr said, "and I felt relief at last to have some family support.

"I returned to Dover a month later, when I felt my daughter was settled in at my mother's home. My family had given me a lot of help and kindness, and I soaked it up and stored it for when the time came to be alone again. There wasn't much money in my purse, but I'd told my family things were fine with me and there was a place for me to stay back in Delaware. Well, that wasn't true, but I found a boat down at a harbor near Baltimore to sleep in for a night or two. The boat hadn't been locked up as tightly as it should have been. I got meals from the eating places for the homeless and received other help from resource centers and missions. I hit them all. Saying I was desperate was an understatement. If anyone spoke kindly to me or offered to help me in any way, I went with them. If I thought I was going nuts, I called the crisis line. Trying to survive became a full-time job. The fact was that several boats were home to me during the first couple of months back in the area. Daring adventures for me—they were unreal. I didn't tell my family how desperate my situation was, because they had helped me enough. My mother didn't need added worries," Starr told me, admitting that she realized what she was up against— the many dangers, hunger, loneliness, exposure, illness, and all the other ugly bedfellows traveling the same roads. She was relying on herself to survive.

I asked Starr two questions—why she had returned to this area instead of remaining in Detroit where she had more opportunities, and why she didn't stay in the shelters. She answered, "I never did like living up north—just never did—and I didn't feel like returning to the shelters at that particular time. I figured I'd meet someone any day that would help me or join with me in finding a place to live."

"In fact, I met a guy named Mike down at the harbor. He talked nice to me and seemed safe to be around. He'd just found a place to live and asked me if I wanted to live with him—it was something like going for a Coke in the 1950s. My mentality was different because of the amount of time I'd lived on the streets and my desperation. It's amazing to me what I've done because of my desperation," she confided. "My sole mission in life is to survive. Since my marriage fell apart, I've always felt like a second-class citizen. I've never expected much from anyone, and I haven't been disappointed—I never got much from anyone. I've since talked with other sisters who have 'wised me up' about street people, and homeless men in particular. I've learned that some men actually make an effort to prey on single and divorced women, especially those who receive government assistance checks on the first of every month. They know how emotionally vulnerable the sisters are. Many of these men slip drugs into the sisters' drinks, con them, threaten them, beat them, lie, cheat and steal." She then offered this advice: "Sisters, you'd better have a heavy anchor out so you won't be swayed by the slick stories and tricks in society's choppy waters. During the first few years of my homelessness, in addition to being naive, I was desperate. Back to my story—I told Mike I'd stay with him for a while, and, if it worked out, I'd bring my daughter back down to live with us.

"Mike and I lived together for about two years, until he started to abuse me. I've found out that live-in relationships are really shaky for women. I've never really known where I stand or what is fair. It's like I'm a pet dog—if I'm good I can stay, but I can't make any messes, can't bark or ruin anything, have to do what I'm told, have to show off for company, can't forget my manners, can't pester him, and always have to remember my place so I won't be dropped off at the pound or in the harbor! Now that's the truth! I always worked when I was with Mike, but it seemed like he was always ridiculing me and belittling my every move. I just felt I never measured up to his expectations. I always seemed to be on probation and under his thumb. I don't know …" she mused.

"I soon discovered Mike was on drugs. I'm not saying I never used them, but I figured I was just on an occasional recreational usage thing. Okay? He went 24–7, which means he wanted to get high twenty-four hours a day, seven days a week. He smoked constantly and was always high. So, you know, I was living with other people off and on. I left him three times but always went back.

"After returning to him the last time, we really got into a terrible fight. I called the cops, and when they arrived I simply asked them to tell my man to keep his hands off me. The next thing I knew the police were arresting me and taking me to jail because I'd been fighting.... They charged me with attempted murder, assault, assault with a deadly weapon, disorderly conduct, and disturbing the peace. Sometimes a person has to strike back when they're in danger of being killed! Mike was the one who had the knife. I just picked it up after he tripped. He told them lies,... and the more he talked the more they wrote. Since he didn't want to file charges, the state filed them. I thought that was totally wrong. They told me the reason they'd filed was because I'd called them on six previous occasions and hadn't pressed charges. There had been new laws passed, and it was mandatory that if the police department was called, and there was evidence of a crime, someone had to be held responsible and arrested. I'd only wanted the cops to scare Mike so he wouldn't smack me again.

"The morning after being admitted into the jail a female attendant showed me a newspaper with my picture in it! I was the first person to enter the big new jail in town. I was not proud, I was horrified! I didn't want anyone knowing I was even in jail! I was so ashamed. I didn't think it was fair that I was the one locked-up in jail. I'd only been defending myself against this man. I'd hurt him, sure, but only after I'd been hurt. I felt sad about hurting him. I really did," she maintained, although I really had no conception of what had happened during this particular altercation.

It seemed that Starr was trying to justify her actions of the time in regard to her incarceration. "There hadn't been an arrest made on any of the previous calls I'd made, and I'd been hurt each of those times; once I thought Mike was going to kill me! On the night of my arrest he'd screamed obscenities, chased me with a knife, thrown me around, hit me in the face several times, kicked me, and finally threw me down some stairs. I may have passed out after landing about halfway down the stairs, but I don't know for sure. I was dizzy and numb and very banged up. When Mike came to pick me up, I hit him and tripped him. He was stoned and fell down the rest of the stairs, and that's when I picked up the knife from him and ran to a phone. Later, he asked me why I'd hit him. I told him to 'get real.' It's not that I didn't have a reason; I had hundreds of reasons. Mike knew what I was talking about," Starr explained.

"Those five months in jail were long, hard months and left me with a lot of time to think. One of my decisions was never to trust anyone again. The law was confusing to me about what rights were mine and what wrongs were Mike's. I'd trusted one officer who'd been to the house before. He acted as though he believed me and would act on what I'd told him. He knew that Mike had severely beaten me many times, because he'd been one of the officers who'd responded to my other calls. He knew first-hand, but I was the only one charged.

"When I was finally in court, the judge asked me, 'How do you plead?' I replied, 'Not guilty, your honor.' My lawyer whispered to me, 'If you plead not guilty, that means we go back to jail and prepare for another trial. You might not win.' She scared me, because I thought I might have to wait another four or five months before receiving another trial date. The judge asked me, again, 'Is this going to be your final plea?' I was very nervous and said, 'no' and then 'yes' and then 'no' again.

The judge became impatient and told my lawyer, 'you tell your client that I want only one answer this time.' I finally said, 'It was self-defense, your honor. I'm not guilty of these charges.'

"My lawyer whispered to me, 'If you want to get out of here, you'll have to plead guilty.' Well, that wasn't right. If I wasn't guilty, why should I say I was? My lawyer and I discussed my options and argued back and forth. Finally, the judge in a very irritated voice said, 'One last time, how are you going to plead?' I finally pleaded guilty, but said it was self-defense.

"The judge then asked, 'Do you understand what you just said?' I just stood there. I finally started to cry and told the judge, 'Just go ahead and do whatever! My man didn't show up in court today and the state pressed the charges. The officer who was at the scene didn't even follow up on anything.' 'Officer, is this true?' the judge asked. The officer answered, 'it's true.' The judge then asked, 'Didn't you even bother going back and check to see if the man was all right?' The officer replied, 'No your honor, there was no follow-up. I was called to the scene. I investigated. I found reason to arrest. The parties involved didn't want to press charges, so the state had to press charges in accordance with the new law.'

"Well," said Starr, "I believe the whole exercise was just to complete the required paperwork down at police headquarters and a formality for case closure. The trouble was, it was at my expense. This was the first time in my life I'd ever been in jail or had any kind of trouble with the law. Some of the charges were dismissed, but I served five months in jail."

Starr shared other experiences she had during her confinement. She announced that she would "never forget the loud noise the heavy metal doors made as I was being locked-up.... My blood ran cold. I thought it was the end of the world for me. In many ways it was. From that moment on, I've never again experienced the feeling of being special. That was the moment in my life when I seemed to lose all innocence, joy, my childlike quality, my specialness, and the possibility of being something wonderful. It might even be termed my magic. Something good did happen to me while in jail, though: doing time made me stop taking drugs. Smoking was not allowed, either, so I quit that bad habit too. Quitting these health and soul-sucking habits didn't really bother me that much, which really surprised me. Mike was the one who did most of the drugs...."

She then informed me: "Many women on the streets are taking some kind of drug—whether it's a prescription drug or sold on the streets. They aren't in any condition to fight deception, or anything else for that matter. These women mix the drugs and it makes them really crazy, if it doesn't just kill them. A homeless woman will take her prescription drugs and then go out. If somebody asks, 'wanna buy or trade some drugs?' she'll answer, 'sure.' This behavior happens mostly on the first few days of each month—right after payday. The food stamps come out at the same time and are traded for drugs. This happens a lot. Every month the cycle repeats itself—hardly any women in the shelters during the first part of the month, and full shelters after the money is gone. The numbers are up and down at the soup kitchens too." She said that some homeless women get together after receiving their government checks, rent a big hotel room, buy drugs, and have a big party. "When everything runs out, back they come to the shelters." Starr believed that if these women would just get together, rent a house, and take care of each other, they could improve their lives. The really sad part is that many of them have children with them.

"Many homeless women have mental or physical problems, or both, from their lifestyle," she claimed. "How could they not? Some are incapable of improving their lives. They talk to themselves out loud and act-out scenes of life as they see them or wish them to be." Many don't even have the level of understanding to fathom the state of their lives and situations. "I've seen them praying to telephone poles, wearing nothing but a blanket as they walk up the street, dress like its Halloween, do crazy things others ask them to do, and even lay down in a public place imagining they're giving birth to a baby," she reported. "Some stack and restack items on grocery store shelves until they are asked to leave. Some dance with imaginary partners." Many blindly follow men who use and abuse the homeless. "Weakness and evil are natural bedmates," she asserted.

"The women who use drugs don't seem or care what's in them or what harm they can cause. These women are at the mercy of everyone, especially the people who handle and sell them drugs.... Women die or become mentally impaired here all the time on account of drug use. They are really crazy from their years of using and from other forms of abuse. Hell, they'll go out and beat up or kill other people to get money for their habits. I've seen many of them after they've been badly beaten—it isn't pretty." I knew that others are sent to mental institutions when they can no longer remember who they are, are unable to recognize friends, can't read, write, or sign their names any longer, or are otherwise unable to care for themselves. "This is the stuff nightmares are made of!" Starr said, having direct knowledge of the drug problems and other abuse in the world of the homeless.

Like many of the homeless women I talked to, Starr happily warned the prospective readers of this book about some special concerns: "Tenants must also be very careful to avoid dangerous situations at the shelters. If a homeless woman has money, or anything else of value when she arrives, she might leave without it. Usually, the women who stay in shelters aren't quite themselves because of abuse, mental anguish, drugs, and for many other reasons. Homeless women staying at the shelters might take advantage of the weaknesses of others. Many of the women will lie, trick, rob, use, and manipulate other tenants, and you must be 'street smart' to survive. Danger and violence aren't very far away when you deal with desperate women. The shelters will supervise and protect as much as they possibly can, but danger is always present," she maintained.

I was surprised when Starr revealed, "I've never actually slept on the streets, but have walked around all night and watched others sleep.

God would never let me go to sleep out there. I believed that if I went to sleep something bad might happen to me. Several guys have threatened me because I wouldn't give them money and refused to do some things they've asked me to do. Others are just so off-the-wall and crazy that you never know what to expect. They can talk fine one minute and then say something that makes no sense at all. A homeless woman must always be on guard."

She then told me more about herself. "My formal education consists of a General Education Diploma. I went to one Job Corps Center and completed a course in electronics and to another center and learned about dietary work. My work experiences haven't been good in this city, though. Maybe I should leave this area. When I've found a good job, some guy usually comes along and sexually harasses me. It's happened more than once. I tell the offenders to stop, but they don't. It's hard to prove sexual harassment, just their word against mine. Who's going to believe me? I'm a jailbird! I do have the courage to turn them in, but I've been the one who got smeared," she said. "No thank you. I've quit the jobs because I just couldn't report to work and suffer the harassment any longer, which, without a steady job, resurrects my homelessness again.

"I was harassed at one company by a man who'd worked there for more than twenty years.... He was such an animal! It wasn't my intention to make him lose his job, but I did want him to leave me alone and not bother me anymore. 'Chester the molester' was the name women at the plant called him, so you just know he had a history of acting out and showing his ass. He was part of upper management in the company, too. Of course, there were never any witnesses other than his victims. He saw to that. He wasn't stupid enough to act out in front of anyone else. He had to have a lot of practice. He was very slick.

"I've learned one thing for sure. A woman has to be a real survivor to make it in this world. Do I report this harassment to the police? I don't think so. I'd found out in the first person about women's rights and jail time. Even if there was a line of women waiting to report this bloody crime against them, and the line reached from Baltimore clear to Washington, D.C., it wouldn't matter," Starr said of this common problem many women face every day in the workplaces in this country and the futility many feel about reporting it. I certainly didn't doubt her basic tale and that she had suffered harassment, but I was beginning to sense that Starr's quitting of jobs or her aggressive complaints against those who she felt had wronged her had perhaps alienated some who might have been able to help her.

Starr's plan for improving her future was through continued education, and she stated, "I'm still going to classes, and right now I'm attending a 'Break the Cycle' employment assistance training program. It takes me nearly three hours each day to get there and return by bus. I plan on getting a certificate from the course. The training I'm receiving now is another building block in my plan to rejoin society in the future. After my classes I walk to a soup kitchen for women called 'Mares Eat Oats.' Down the road I can see myself working for an electronics company. Maybe I'll even teach others about electronics. I have other talents, too. I've told you that I played in a band with Willie. I play drums and keyboard by ear and may use my musical talents in addition to a regular job.

"Many years have passed since Willie and I parted company and our family life has changed considerably. He's where he is. I'm where I am. I'm still homeless, and Melody is still living with my mother. She's better off there. Would you believe she's twelve years old now? My so-called husband lived with his momma for more than a year after we left. I could have gone back and lived with him after a few years if I'd wanted to, but I just couldn't forget what he'd done to me and Melody. What kind of a man would let his wife and child live in shelter after shelter and not even make an attempt to help them? I've lost too much respect for him to ever want to be close to him again or have a repeat performance of the big letdown. I'm forty-two years old now, but sometimes the wedding ceremony seems like it was yesterday. Here comes the bride, oh, how she's cried, and tried, and died! I sometimes wonder what snapped in me after Willie and his momma threw me out. Sometimes I look back to the time when I had a respectable job and was enthusiastic about getting ahead. I never even realized what homelessness was, or thought about it. Sometimes I forget about the woman I used to be and am shocked at how I ended up on the streets … and have stayed on them year in and year out. I was surprised when I learned that Willie had bought a home in the same area where my mother and daughter live. I believe someday I'll probably go back up north, even though I don't like it there. Maybe I'll settle in Cleveland or Columbus. They're fine. Who knows where I'll end up? I don't," Starr said, as she reminisced about the changes she and her family have gone through.

Her pride was evident as Starr expressed her feelings about working at the day shelter. "I enjoy my volunteer work here. I do my best to make this a better place for the homeless women in this city. The Catholic church has been wonderful to countless women who are in transition. I shower and dress here each morning, and work several hours each week helping with whatever needs to be done. They trust me here. I'm a hard worker. At one time or another, I've stayed in most of the shelters in this area, and I am very grateful for the comfort they provided me. The shelter where I've been staying just closed for the summer, but I've found another place to stay.

"I've met a new guy, but we're just friends, that's all," she confided. "He lives just around the corner from here, and I feel that rooming at his place for a while will help me out in the long run. I'll stay there until I can get a job and afford a place of my own. I hope it won't be long until a good opportunity presents itself. I've met different men who've helped guide me to job training. The problem is that they think because they've helped me I owe them some kind of favor or permanent commitment. I just want them as friends, that's all. Why can't men understand that about women without us having to sound ugly by reminding them? We help them with their problems, too, and encourage them to have better lifestyles. I don't expect anything in return. I'm sorry if that isn't satisfactory. These guys will just have to find willing women who want a commitment of the kind they have in mind. I give guys the inspiration to improve, but that's all I want to give them," she maintained.

Starr continued her talk about men. "If a man wants to be with me, he must have a good job and a promising future. Anyway, most of the time the guy straightens up, goes out and gets himself a good job, and then realizes that I really don't want him for a permanent companion. I've always been up-front with men. When I help people, it makes me feel good. I talk to them, listen to their stories, and do favors for them. I'm a good listener and a good friend. I want three things in my life from people: respect, understanding, and for them to be responsible people. People have to put forth effort if they want to be around others who put forth effort.

"You've probably heard the term 'opposites attract.' Well, I'm here to tell you that it might be true, but only for a while. I think that the more one has in common with a partner the better their chances are for getting along. I've found that many guys on the streets cherish material things instead of a loved one. They should be in love with someone instead of something. I know a lot of guys out there who are more interested in material possessions, habits, hobbies, and sporting activities than they are in their women and families. We sisters need to say, 'Move on brother and get yourself another!'

"I'm not addicted to anything except real love now. Please don't break my heart. I've tried to give my love to men before and they just smacked me one to the head! This is the city of deception; it's not the city of charm. Some men come at you really charming, but all the while it's deception. Most of them love to flirt too, or talk trash. I know that flirting is just another way of saying, 'I'd love to be with you.' If their talk is trash, well, that's probably what they think you are too! Watch out for this type of guy! But I figure it's a lot like alcohol … three days after it's worn off the deception shows up. It's not fair that people misrepresent themselves. It's not honest. Of course, the bad types aren't honest to begin with, and probably don't even know what the word means. The sooner the sisters realize this, the further they're ahead in the game. Some sisters say, 'so what if I didn't win the big prize, I had fun playing the games.' Well, sisters, I'm tired of playing the games. We women always seem to come out the losers," Starr said, voicing feelings drawn from her personal experiences and interactions with other street people.

"At the last shelter where I stayed I had to get up at five o'clock each morning and leave. There were no meals served there, so losing weight was easy. If I don't have a good breakfast, though, the day doesn't really get off to a good start and I haven't the energy to walk the streets and look for work. I'm half sick most of the time. Lunch has never been that important to me, but a good breakfast is a must," Starr explained.

"I've been inspired and helped so much by the good people here at the day shelter, and have tried to pay them back for their kindness to me," she continued. "One of my service goals is to help with projects that will make this a better place. Each day there is something all of us can do to help each other improve our lives. The homeless women come here to relax, rest, shower, have coffee, visit, use the phone, write letters, have snacks, stuff like that. Just having a place to get off the streets is a gift. I'm very proud of the things I've done here, especially helping with the mural we painted outside on the wall. It shows our homeless sisters being watched over and protected by guardian angels. There are hope and glory shown. On the far right is a skeleton, which represents life and death, and is symbolic of the sisters who didn't make it in this world as a result of freezing to death on the streets, starvation, murder, illness, loneliness, exposure, or simply from a broken heart. I truly believe we have guardian angels watching over us. On the far left of the mural are figures representing the young and old. There is no age discrimination in homelessness. Looking at our mural can't help but make you aware of the struggles many women face."

Starr's comments and obvious pride and joy in the mural were revealing and heartwarming to me. She then volunteeered more information: "The art lady from the Catholic Charities and her husband drew the layout for the mural, and the homeless sisters here painted it. Which reminds me to say something about the art lady's husband. What a wonderful, wonderful man. I wish there were millions more men just like him. This world would be a heaven in no time at all. Of course, maybe the art lady is smarter about picking her man. Oh well, back to the project. The project took about six weeks to complete. Those who stayed with the project from beginning to end were awarded certificates and had a party given in their honor," Starr reported.

"How would you like to be remembered, Starr?" I asked her. She concluded our interview by saying, "I'd like to be remembered as a caring, kind, loving, responsible, intelligent, and successful woman. I keep telling myself that my homeless state is 'temporary,' but it can't last much longer or it will consume the rest of my life. My counselors keep asking me, 'If not now, when, will you leave the streets?'"

I truly hoped she would be successful in escaping her life of homelessness and shelters. I thought of Starr's wishes when I read Ralph Waldo Emerson's description of the keys to a successful life: "To laugh often and love much; to win the respect of intelligent persons and the affection of children. To leave the world a bit better, whether by a healthy child, a garden patch or a redeemed social condition. To know that even one life has breathed easier because you have lived. This is to have success."

* * *

Eighteen months after our interview, I called the day shelter to see how Starr was doing and was told that she was still working there. She came to the phone and told me that she was involved in a new art project. The "art lady" and her husband from Catholic Charities asked each woman at the shelter to draw a picture of the flower that best represented themselves. When they have finished, the flowers will be transposed onto a layout and become part of a mural depicting a beautiful garden. This new mural will be painted on an outside wall of a building close to the shelter. I somewhat mischievously asked Starr if she thought there would be any weeds in the garden. She replied, "not if I can help it!"

I sometimes wonder if Starr will ever leave the day center and the streets. It is her home during the daytime hours, and at night she leaves as if going on a date or to a party at someone's place. It's funny how our minds can accept our circumstances after a while and makes the best of our situation, whether by fantasizing or other rationales. I have heard that sometimes people who live in confinement, such as in jails or prisons, become "institutionalized." They are afraid to live on their own again. Some people at the shelters and on the streets perhaps are much the same, as they adopt others of this lifestyle as their family and the shelters as their home. Whether she ultimately leaves or not, for now, at least, the work at the shelter is meaningful to Starr and she is helpful to others. I believe that, for the most part, she feels complete.

Isabelle

W HEN I FIRST WAS INTRODUCED to her, Isabelle was working at the front desk of a women's shelter in Montana. She was just completing her work requirement as a tenant at the shelter. I told her my reason for being at the shelter and asked if she'd consent to do an interview with me and tell me about her homelessness. I was delighted when she consented. Her shift was just ending, and she asked me to follow her to a conference room where we could speak in private. I noticed that she walked with a pronounced limp and grimaced in pain each time she took a step. I wondered if her physical condition might have some connection with her homelessness.

Isabelle was a fifty-two-year-old homeless Hispanic woman. She began her story directly and with no hesitation. "Nineteen years ago I began working at a large plant in southern California. My life was good. My old Spanish neighborhood was a pleasure to live in, especially since most of my family was close by. My health was good. I was happy. One day I decided to go for a ride on a motorcycle, and life as I'd known it was no more. Years of surgeries and pain followed, but I did my best to carry on. Just before I was eligible for retirement, I was bequeathed a pink slip from the company. I felt bitter about the layoff, and my perception of the general workplace was one of deception and unfairness."

Isabelle seemed very intelligent, if somewhat outspoken. Her account continued. "I moved to Montana from Los Angeles in May 1993, just to get on with my life, not to retire or become homeless. As I told you, my position was cut after nineteen years of loyal service, just one year shy of retirement. For me, this was 'the unkindest cut of all!' I'd

144

just wanted to work another year and be eligible for my retirement—not an unreasonable desire. I'm one of those people who'd done everything right to ensure a good life and retirement, but eventually I found myself on the streets. I'm living proof that accidents can and do happen every day that can ruin or debilitate a person and prevent them from living a normal lifestyle. One lesson I learned from my layoff experience was that I should have been more aware about the 'lapse clause' in my health insurance contract. I should have found out everything I could about handicap and disability benefits sooner rather than later.

"I truly believe that women must place a greater emphasis on a good health insurance program for ourselves, whether we live alone or with a partner. It must be at the top of our priority list when accepting a position—above salary, above vacation time, above status symbols, and even above retirement benefits. We must all make sure that we have a total health-care package. Another benefit that should concern us would be that company money is provided for retraining in another skill or trade when a layoff occurs. Take it or leave it, that's my best advice to you. Unless, of course, you don't mind living on the streets."

Isabelle's counsel certainly seemed sound to me, and I determined that I would include it in this book. It was further emphasized by her own unfortunate experience. I was learning much from this woman, who went on with her story. "At least I was able to face my immediate future thanks to the remnants of my 401K plan and severance pay from the company. It wasn't like I just let go. I'd done nearly everything possible to prepare for an emergency. I had what I considered to be adequate health and life insurance, although it didn't turn out that way. I had seniority rights in my company, and saved the maximum money allowed in my 401K account, which was 10 percent of my pay, matched once a year by the company. I believe that is why they let me go: I was costing them too much money! It makes me angry that companies get away with treating their employees so unfairly. I now realize that I probably could have done a lot more to prepare for my 'rainy day,' but I'm not going to beat myself up any more. I'm satisfied that I did as much as I knew how to do. Sure, I've got regrets, but, hey, I've just got to cut my losses and begin again. I feel that none of my troubles were really my fault, and, no, I'm not in total denial! I didn't cause the layoff, and I didn't cause the accident that has destroyed my leg. Those happenings weren't fair to me, but I've discovered that the sooner in life a person learns that sometimes life isn't fair, the better.

She claimed that she had managed to save nearly $40,000 in her 401K plan, but that the government "took half of that for taxes and penalties. Most of my savings went for medical costs and expenses just to keep me alive and afloat during a rough financial time for me. The motorcycle accident eight years earlier had left me nearly unable to walk. It was necessary for me to use crutches to get around at home and at work—a wheelchair was never an option for me, because I simply refused to use one. I had nine surgeries and two bone grafts, and a diagnosis of osteomyelitis came as no surprise to me because of all the complications and problems I'd experienced. To this day, I don't know whether or not I'm going to be able to keep my leg. I'm really physically disabled. The medications are very expensive, but without them I'd lose my leg or my life," Isabelle said. She related how sometimes the excruciating pain in her leg makes moving it almost unbearable. She also commonly runs a high fever and, more often than not, does not have a general feeling of well-being.

Isabelle spoke next about some earlier events in her life. "I remember the company Christmas party in 1991 before the big layoff came down. The owner of the company came to cheer us peasants on.... What a guy!" Isabelle said sarcastically. "I thought he was on drugs, myself, because I don't believe I would ever have chosen to say what he had in front of 2,000 employees who hadn't had a pay increase in a couple of years and many of them facing a layoff. He told them, 'I understand what it feels like to be poor, because I just took nineteen people to the Caribbean for Thanksgiving!' Now, wasn't that a statement! The party was over at 1:30 p.m., but none of the employees returned to work that day. They felt a lot of hostility toward the company and I didn't blame them for leaving. I thought, 'What is he, a fool?' He'd insulted the shop workers ... the bread and butter of the company, and they were proud of the fine work they had done."

Isabelle not only had felt threatened by a possible layoff at work but also by the unrest in Los Angeles during the spring of 1992. She said, "There were a lot of crimes being committed and the violence and rioting were intense. I'd never experienced anything like the events of this period, and couldn't believe the fury in the United States of America. The employees of our company were told not to return to work until things quieted down. I felt isolated and alone as I listened to calls for the LAPD on a police scanner. Life was really scary. One night I heard a woman call the cops for help. The dispatcher told her, 'Honey, we don't have any more cops to send!' I was frightened out of my wits! Right after that call, I heard loud engine noises outside my home, and when I looked out the window I saw tanks and military personnel coming up the street! It was a scene from hell! I screamed, 'God, I'm alone, please help me!' I weathered that particular danger, but felt forsaken and somewhat helpless going about my daily life."

She then revealed details about her layoff from work during that period. "It was a dark day in July of 1992 when my termination paper was given to me. I took care of matters at hand after my layoff ... most important things first. The condition of my leg was worsening and the doctors were suggesting amputation, but I said no. A team of specialists decided the next best course for me would be to have an operation on my leg. It took months to complete the insurance paperwork qualifying me for the special procedure, and my health insurance with the company lapsed just before the paperwork was approved. With no health insurance, I couldn't afford the operation or the $1,000 a month for the prescriptions I needed. I'd spent most of the money I'd saved on medical and living expenses.

"Moving was a decision I didn't want to make, but at that time it seemed to me that I was forced to do so. I'd lost my house because I fell behind on my mortgage payments. I had to put my furniture in storage after losing my house, and when storage costs couldn't be paid I lost my furniture and other possessions. I was in a state of constant panic, anxiety, and pain. What was I going to do? Where would I go? I had checked the crime rate in other cities located along the coast and it was high in those places too. Los Angeles and the San Fernando Valley were no longer the wonderful places I'd known as a child. I'd loved my old historic Spanish community and the feeling of tranquility there. Where had the music, the great food, the dancing, the singing, and the laughter in the streets gone? The great legacy handed down from our early Spanish settlers was in great danger of disappearing. Each day, as I hobbled down the streets on my crutches, I found myself wondering whether the people walking toward me were going to harm me or kill me. It was time to leave. I'm not a paranoid type of a person, but safety is something to be considered at all times. How sad. I couldn't kid myself. My sacred ground was shrinking," Isabelle stated, reliving some of the anguish she had felt at the time.

She continued: "Being in a bind and in a state of limbo wasn't the route I wanted to continue on, so I made my decision. My brother was living in Montana and he seemed very happy there, so I decided to go to 'Big Sky Country' to see if I could improve my lot in life. I'd heard the lifestyle was good there, and I had to move somewhere. It took a lot out of me to get ready and actually make the move." It wasn't clear to me if Isabelle lived with her brother for a while or immediately obtained employment and was able to rent a place of her own. I chose to remain silent in hope that her story would become more clear in the telling. Some aspects didn't, unfortunately, but I became engrossed in her tale and my interruptions were minimal.

"Eighteen months after arriving in Montana my life went completely bad. I made the wrong choice for a roommate. A male answered my newspaper ad to share space in the house I'd rented. There was room for two separate dwellings, and the agreement was strictly to share expenses; however, soon after he moved in, he moved his girl-friend into his living space. I didn't like this arrangement because they were noisy and there was no place for me to relax after working all day. I'd lost my privacy."

She described her search for work. "I found several jobs in Montana, but, unfortunately, there were no major companies or corporations in the area, and the available jobs didn't provide medical benefits. In October 1993 I was told confidentially by a personnel manager that I had several strikes against me in getting hired by businesses in town. I was more than forty years old, a woman, and didn't know any influential people. Well, I resented this discrimination immensely and said so, for all the good it did me," Isabelle said angrily.

"The work I did find at a local school was too physical for me, and when I'd come home at night I was miserable for the rest of the evening. My health was deteriorating because the work was wearing me down. All the fun and joy were missing from my life. I was so preoccupied with pain and worry that I couldn't enjoy myself," she revealed. In January 1994 I got a job at a casino. I liked working there, but management short-changed me on my hours. I could deal with the reduced wages to a point, but I had to find a way to get food. Eating at St. Vincent DePaul every day saved me, because there was only enough money in my purse to pay rent and put gas in my car. I only used my car to go eat, go back and forth to work, and to hunt for a better job. St. Vincent DePaul is the greatest place, and going there quieted my anxiety ... just knowing I wasn't going to starve to death helped me a lot," she confided, and I was pleased that she had some good to say about some organization, although I did not doubt that she had suffered injustices. It seemed that her bitterness over the accident and her first layoff had colored her reaction to other life situations.

She continued her story. "A new casino was opening in town, so I submitted my application. I spoke to one of the ladies working at the casino. She was at least sixty years old and knew the overall management of the casino. I respected her. She said to me, 'I'll tell you something right now, honey, they won't hire you no matter how good you are.' 'Why is that?' I asked her. She answered, 'You're not young.' Now, that was the second time I'd heard this statement made in town. I knew this hiring policy was absolutely against the law, not to mention against good judgment. Older people will be on the job every day, in all kinds of weather, busting their butts, doing anything that's asked of them," Isabelle said, becoming more and more animated.

"All work and no play was definitely making me a person cut off from the celebrations of life. I was tired of being apart from other people, and decided to accept an invitation to a party during the holiday season. I was excited about being asked to go out on New Year's Eve, and looked forward to the evening. I usually don't drink at all, especially since I'm on several medications. However, on that particular evening I had some drinks too. It was the beginning of the end of my independence. When I got home from the party, my roommate was drunk and out of control. I immediately saw that my car had been severely damaged. The windshield was broken and there were dents over the entire car. When I walked into my part of the house, I saw that the walls were damaged, my pictures and keepsakes were broken, and all kinds of other destruction was evident. I exploded! I knew my roommate had done it because he had become more and more antagonistic of late and had threatened me during various confrontations we'd had. I approached him about the damage and he became physically violent. One thing led to another, and before long the neighbors notified the police. When the law arrived, we were both arrested. I said to the cops, 'What can I say, you got me!' The police charged me with 'disorderly conduct, brought on by alcohol.'

"I'd never been in trouble with the law before and was totally devastated by my arrest. I couldn't believe this had happened to me. Old wounds needed to be healed, not new ones opened. My home was where my heart was, and was supposed to be a nice, safe place for me to meditate and heal. Well, my heart was broken, my place was a mess, and I was under arrest. Happy New Year!

Isabelle then cataloged a list of problems, including fines and conditions of her parole. Not everything made sense, however; and it seemed clear that she saw herself as a victim, not explaining her part in the situations. "It was January 1, 1995, and at that point in my life my thinking wasn't clear for a lot of reasons. I felt that I'd lost everything I cared about. I had to give away my dog and my cat, who were like children to me, since I'd never had any. I'd been evicted. My health was deteriorating. I was in debt and had no money in the bank. My nice car was ruined, and I'd temporarily lost my freedom. I knew that my life needed to change. I also knew that I needed my freedom, not just from jail, but from the pain I'd endured for so long, and from the worries that had followed me for the last several years. My Lord, I was tired. I wanted to feel well enough to make the positive changes needed to improve my life. I was haunted by the consequences of my actions, but felt I'd been driven to that point by my roommate and the general circumstances in my life. I've learned many lessons and paid dearly for them. Right then and there while in that detention facility, I promised myself from that time forth I would choose my friends and roommates more carefully—friends who shared my same interests—and together we would help and care for each other," she explained.

"I stayed with my brother and his family after my ordeal. There was no one else to turn to for help. My family support group had been fractured twenty years earlier when my mother had been murdered. Her death had devastated me. The trial was unbelievable, and the verdict was hard to accept. She had an existing heart problem, so the courts didn't charge her assailant with murder. He was only fourteen years old, and I understand that in some cases age might require a different type of trial. However, I hold the courts responsible for the injustice in my mother's death, because that boy had been before a judge or in the system at least ten times before he killed mama. Someone should have said, 'Hey, there's a problem with this boy's behavior; we need to take some steps to make sure the public is protected.' But again, someone in the legal system dropped the ball. After the verdict was read, my brother yelled, 'Let me beat him in the head ten times with a brick and see if his heart stops!'

"A person who kills can be out of detention in less than five years, while people who commit other types of crimes of a lesser violence can serve up to fifteen years," Isabelle said. "It doesn't make any sense. Until we get our courts and judges to put some bite into the penalties, there'll be sharks out there blending in with the general public. If you get a twelve-year sentence, then, damn it, you should serve twelve years! There's also a difference between a first-time offense, which might possibly have been an accident, and an offender with multiple convictions. Many times the jury doesn't even get to hear about prior convictions. Maybe judges should take an oath to let the truth, the whole truth, and nothing but the whole truth be told, so help them God!" Isabelle exclaimed.

"I'm happy that I don't live in Los Angeles anymore. L.A.'s not fine, and it ain't my home no more! There was so much violence when I was there, and the courts forgot who the real victims were much of the time. My California is a sad state of affairs," Isabelle said. She then voiced some of her opinions on growing up and the role of discipline in raising children.

"Looking back, I didn't have the best of childhoods, but because I grew up poor did I go around hating, destroying, or killing people? No, I did not. I understand that bad things happen sometimes, but, for the most part, we all choose what we do. People choose to steal, to drink, to cheat, to lie, to hurt, and there's always a price to pay. I believe that being polite and having good manners is something you instill in children as they are growing up. We were a poor family, but my parents taught us to show respect for other people's feelings and possessions. They spanked us when we had it coming; but to hear us holler you'd have thought they were killing us. In retrospect, it was nothing. We got spanked for misbehaving. We didn't get beaten. If we didn't get spanked, we stood in a corner.

"Today, children are lucky to have both parents. Sometimes parents today just let disrespect and misbehavior go unpunished because they're afraid of being charged with child abuse. Some programs and commercials on radio and television teach children to disrespect their parents and elders. The children respond by thinking it's cool to be a smart-aleck and believe they're supposed to act the same as the characters act on screen. It's unfortunate, and I've worked side by side with people who I would have thought had the best upbringing, but I've got to tell you that I've been blown away by stories they've told me about what their parents did to them, or how their parents died. In retrospect, I had it easy. I would change nothing. I was taught right from wrong and how to be respectful. I was treated fairly as a child," Isabelle said matter-of-factly. Later, I came across some words of Anne Frank that would have been nice to share with Isabelle: "Parents can only give good advice or put them on the right paths, but the final forming of a person's character lies in their own hands."

Isabelle's own story continued. "When I was in the mental health and DUI classes, I asked the people in charge, 'Why do people come here over and over again? I can see once, maybe even twice; but coming here three, four, and five times is absolutely ridiculous. Why would the courts send somebody here that many times?' I was told, 'If you don't like it, you change the way it is!' Well, hey, somebody had a deal going there and it wasn't me! I was grateful they busted me and that I hadn't hurt anyone. It was stupid for me to go out and drink and drive, and lose control of my temper, but it is also stupid that the state runs liquor stores. I usually believe in 'live and let live,' but when it infringes upon my rights, my safety, and my taxes, then I have to be concerned. I hold judicial officials accountable for our tax dollars they are spending, and also the sentences they are issuing. If the officials don't make the grade, give them the boot!" Those last statements made even more clear my feeling that Isabelle's strong opinions and confrontational attitude had probably contributed to her problems.

Isabelle had been concerned about where she would live after getting out of jail. She related, "I finally decided I'd have to live with my brother and his family. I tried to pull my weight with the chores and expenses, but I didn't have much money and I knew that I would have to get some kind of financial help soon. I needed medication to save my life. I used to drive by this shelter and thought it was nice that people had a decent place to come when they are homeless. I finally decided to call the shelter in February 1995, just to see what they had to offer and to find out what I needed to do to get into the program. I asked them, 'What if I have a job?' I was told, 'If you're unable to pay for living quarters, you're considered homeless.'

"I couldn't believe I actually qualified for a shelter!" she exclaimed. "It wasn't like some places where you have a place to sleep only temporarily—a place to eat a few meals—and after that you're on your own again. I'd thought about sleeping on the streets, but I just couldn't do it. I was worried about my leg infections, and knew I had to have professional help immediately to avoid amputation and further complications. On Easter Sunday, while visiting at a friend's house, I realized that this was to be the day I would go to the shelter. I cried as I wrote the goodbye note to my brother. He still doesn't know where I am; I'm too ashamed to contact him. I had finally let go of my struggle to survive on my own. As Sophie Tucker once said, 'Just Keep Breathing,' and that's what I'm doing. I'd thought that tolerating my pain and working steadily, even though it was for a wage that wasn't enough to live on, just plugging along, was the right way to go, but I finally realized that I needed more help than I could get by doing it my way," Isabelle related, sharing this painful episode in her life.

"I've always worked and made good money, never dreaming that at fifty years old I'd be homeless. Being homeless is something a woman doesn't think about when she's working and has security. This is a whole new ball game for me. People don't fully understand and just automatically assume that because a person is in a homeless situation they've done bad things in their lives. Not true. But again, I do see women and families who come here to the shelter and it's a way of life for them. This shouldn't happen. Homelessness should be as temporary as a person can make it. Women can be living in expensive homes or apartments, driving a new car, wearing nice clothes, and think they're doing very well. Then something unexpected occurs: the big layoff, illness, death of a family member, or another kind of catastrophe," Isabelle said, describing circumstances that can lead many people from a sheltered environment to the streets.

Isabelle then described what it was like for her at the shelter. "When I arrived at this shelter, I was given a room with a bed. It is strange how much those two things mean to a person when you have neither. My heart swelled with love for the people who gave me both. Another homeless woman occupied the room too, and I wound up on the top bunk. Well, let me tell you, I'm not light in weight nor good of leg and didn't want to be up there very long. My goal was to sleep in a bed that was on the floor. The woman who bunked with me was a certified manic depressive and it was a hard week with her because at times she was just off the wall. She screamed all night long, 'save me, save me, get me out of here!' I felt sorry for her, because I too suffered pain, only of a different type. Her type of behavior was hard to tolerate, though. Fortunately, coming from Los Angeles, I'd learned how to deal with different kinds of people. There's a place here in town where people can go if they're poor and have mental problems, and, by doing so, more shelter space is available here for people who are just homeless."

Isabelle continued by saying, "I'm so thankful for what this program affords me. There are special people here at the shelter who can differentiate between the con artists, the way-of-lifers, and those individuals who are truly needy. I hated to ask for help, but the relief I feel from having done so is lifting my burdens day by day. Thank God for these people. Without this shelter and its health care program, and without St. Vincent DePaul, I'd be dying or already dead," she claimed. "One has to appreciate this help. In the past three months I've been very ill. Two weeks ago the doctor wanted to put me in the hospital, but I'm limited as to how many vouchers I can get to help me. I didn't have quite enough of them to go to the hospital, but I did have enough to fill two prescriptions. The medicine is very expensive, but it keeps the infection under control," Isabelle maintained.

"For a long time after arriving at this shelter I was in total denial of my homelessness. 'Just misplaced,' I considered myself. Gradually, I realized how desperate I was and asked the supervisors and nurses about what options were available to me for help. They suggested I apply for disability benefits from the government. I looked into the qualifications of the program and learned that review and approval for a disability request could take from several months to a year. I've applied for the benefits and am now awaiting approval. Nurse practitioners come to the shelter twice a week. If they aren't sure of the medical condition of the tenant, they refer them to a specialist. In my case, an orthopedic doctor was recommended and approved to examine and provide medical care for me. I've also been able to get dental work and eyeglasses. I'm a proud person and it was hard for me to ask for these helps. I can't believe how good it feels to receive what I so desperately needed. They were gifts that lifted my burdens and spirit."

Isabelle then mentioned how her spirits were improving and other psychological benefits she was receiving. "Even living here now and working at the front desk, I try to understand the rules, limitations of the program, availability of items and help, how to deal with different types of personalities and habits, and many other things. I must say, my disposition has improved considerably. I'm finally losing my negativity. I've tried to make the best of my circumstances, whether it's my disability or some other setback. Sometimes living with a group of strangers is hard. If I'm bothered by them, I just go to my room or take a walk. You never know how some of the residents are going to react to the different situations that arise here. This is like a big, old tenement home, and no two people are alike. Sometimes they just stay the night. We constantly get calls from the police, churches, hospitals, and the bus depot referring people to our shelter.

"I no longer have to share a room, because I've earned privileges by working. I now have my own bed, linens, shower, toilet, and a television in my room. I live in real luxury. I'm serious, that's how I feel," Isabelle said, explaining her progress as a resident, and expressing genuine appreciation for what she received. She then further explained what life was like at the shelter.

"One requirement for being a resident is that you either pay three dollars a night or do a two-hour chore, such as working in the laundry, cleaning the shelter, working on the desk, or whatever else needs to be done. The tenants staying here are responsible for maintaining the shelter. Everyone has to do something to keep the shelter up to standard, or it will be closed. After I arrived here, I stopped working in the general work force; however, I didn't have the money to pay my fines for my New Year's Eve celebration, so I made arrangements to do community service in place of my fines. Aside from that, I don't have any other real financial obligations. Up until last week I was working about forty hours a week on the front desk, but I couldn't work all night here at the shelter and then work elsewhere all the next day doing community service. Sometimes when a person is physically run down the mental part goes too. I'm fortunate that there are a couple of really nice people here that I can laugh and have fun with while I'm working. The trouble is that people come and go and you can't make lasting friendships. I long for things that last as I get older," Isabelle confided.

She took her duties at the front desk seriously. "Violent people and others with addictions of one substance or another come to the shelter and request to stay. We must decide whether or not they can be admitted. If a person seems questionable, we don't let them in. We have no choice but to turn them away if there are signs of violent behavior or obvious evidence of substance abuse. These are rules that must be observed in order to protect the residents and the shelter. An alarm system warns a residential house staff member when there is an emergency. If a resident comes down to the desk and says he or she wants to go to the hospital, we can't just open the door. Of course, if the problem is obvious, like profuse bleeding or some other acute condition, there's never a question. We also have a warning system that will bring the police immediately. Sometimes people get angry at us when we require that certain standards are met, but we can't jeopardize the shelter," Isabelle explained, displaying a real dedication to protect the shelter that had given her so much.

"One thing I've learned is not to hesitate if I see trouble, because hesitation can cost someone their life. Recently a couple with four children came into the shelter and another resident heard the man being boisterous after the family was in their room. The resident also heard what sounded like children being beaten. Members of our staff immediately went up and asked the man to take a test to detect alcohol. When he refused, he received an immediate resident termination. That type of behavior is never tolerated. There are other types of destructive behavior that happen here, including destruction of property, theft, verbal abuse, and violence against other tenants. The rooms here are nice, but some individuals choose to destroy the place.

"Though this is only a temporary shelter, if after thirty days a resident needs to stay longer, she can be placed in a variety of special programs," Isabelle continued. "I just finished a program about financing and budgeting. It was called 'Tax Shelters for the Indigent.' Only joking. The instructor taught us basic skills, such as making a budget, balancing a checkbook, smart shopping, and finding affordable housing. Most of the women in the class were intelligent and knew how to perform these tasks. Even though I felt I didn't really need the class, I took it," proclaimed Isabelle, who seemed to be consciously trying to improve her situation.

"Now that I've been here for a while, I've started to come to terms with the reality of my situation. The program has offered me a lot, but it has been a very difficult period in my life. When I go to bed at night I feel safe and can rest and heal. Other than my illness, most of my problems are financial, and if I get the government disability I should be fine. I'm getting older, so I'd better find the right solutions to my problems or I'll be homeless forever, and, with my health, forever won't last long," Isabelle confided.

"Working on the front desk gives me an opportunity to meet a lot of people as they come in for help. One of the things I've learned is how many of these people have been all over the United States. Living in shelters is basically what they do; they know no other way of life.

Some of the homeless are demanding and unappreciative, playing the system for everything they can get. Their attitude really bothers me. At times I've come close to telling them what I think about their attitude, but I can't—it's against the rules. I believe attitude is acquired in a person's upbringing. I've heard some tenants say, 'this shelter is not as good as the shelter we had in this place or that place.' I try not to judge or condemn them. This is my first time around, and hopefully my last. As I've said before, I'm grateful for the help I've received here.

"I had religion in my life as a young child, but it kind of got away from me as the years went by. We have religious training here at the shelter, and one of the rules of the program is that after being here for thirty days it's mandatory that a tenant goes to church on Sunday. In addition to the weekend service, we have chapel on Monday and Thursday, too. If we attend church somewhere other than the chapel here, we have to walk, so that's out of the question for me. There's a van to take us out for medical or emergency purposes, but we don't have funding available for transportation to and from other activities. Many people may joke about my next statement, but I don't care, it's true. I'm closer to God since I came here. I go to Bible study once a week and also to chapel services. I look forward to these studies. I've always had God in my heart, but I didn't always do what I was supposed to do. I go to the Salvation Army church, which I really enjoy. The first time I attended I could have sworn the sermon was about me! I wondered how the preacher knew so much about my personal life. Laugh if you want, but living a churchgoing life is the way I want to go. I feel good when I'm there.

"Two weeks after attending my first church service I took my best friend with me. Half an hour into the service I looked at her and tears were flowing down her cheeks. I asked her why she was crying, and she said, 'He's saying a lot.' 'Do you know the difference between you and me?' I asked her. 'You've got the Kleenex!' she said.

I laughed with her. It was good for me to hear about these positive changes in Isabelle's life. Even her attitude had changed as she discussed the shelter and the joy she found in church. "I'm glad I've gotten reacquainted with the Lord. I go happily. I'm learning to use the Bible, but I'm slow and always cheat—I find my answers in the index. A little sinning there, I know," Isabelle confessed.

"I live by the rules of the shelter and try to pull my weight. There are so many nice people doing nice things here, and I don't want to be the one who brings it all down. It's my new start. I can't praise the people of Montana enough who have shared their talents and harvest with us. One schoolteacher comes here once a week and teaches arts and crafts, especially to the little children. He even brings his own supplies, which is really great. He came last Thursday afternoon and brought us lots of Swiss and American cheese, several pounds of ham, turkey, and roast beef. He'd given a party and had leftovers and thought we might enjoy the food. You better believe we did. . . .

"The shelter furnishes hot food twice a day. Sometimes it's good and sometimes it isn't; but, like I've learned, it's better than nothing, and it's something in your stomach. Some residents are negative about the food, but my attitude is, 'Hey, there's peanut butter and jelly on the table, shut your mouth!' The shelter relies on donations from different sources. Sometimes we get game meat from the men's mission, and they don't always have the best of cooks over there. We get a lot of potatoes and vegetables, and even milk periodically, along with bread and a lot of pastries from different stores in town. One group of people had a party the other night and there were dozens of hoagie sandwiches left over, so they gave them to us. I can't say 'thank you' enough for all the little kindnesses people have given us. It means a lot. Here in Montana people eat a lot of game meat, like elk, moose, venison, and buffalo, so we are given a lot of this type of meat. Some residents complain and say the meat is a road kill, but the majority of us are thankful. I get so upset by the attitude of some of the residents, because when people have been really hungry, like many of us have been, we truly appreciate these offerings. Besides, what are the complainers contributing to society? Nothing good that I can see.

"We depend upon public support for personal items also, such as toilet paper, toothpaste, shampoo, diapers, and those personal sort of things. Everything is donated. If there are no contributions, we don't have the items and people just have to do without," Isabelle reported.

After finally letting go of what wasn't working for her, Isabelle took the advice of her counselors and investigated her options. "I checked with the state social services office to see what programs I was eligible for, and found that I only qualified for the food stamp program. I've paid government taxes for more than thirty-two years and made a lot of money, and because I'm a single person, I was hit with outrageous taxes," she lamented, feeling that she had been shortchanged by the system. Now, I wouldn't be able to live if it wasn't for this shelter. Many women who have worked long and hard don't qualify for any of the programs. I do fall under the federal 'disabled' category, as I've said before. However, it takes a long time for the paperwork to make its way through the red tape and bureaucracy. I'll be able to make it on my own, though, when I'm approved. It isn't fair, and doesn't make much sense, that even though a woman has paid into the system her whole work life she can't get anything back out of it, while a woman who has never worked, nor paid taxes, gets all the benefits of the programs with little or no effort. Changes should be made to provide for the really needy women who have no means of supporting themselves, but the help should be temporary if she is able to work and improve her life."

After sharing her ideas about the system, Iabelle talked a bit about other homeless women and some of the survival strategies they used. "There's a Native American woman who comes around here and tells her story. Before her husband's death they were like two peas in a pod and had everything they could ever want or imagine. Then her husband died of alcoholism and she lost everything and found herself on the streets. Now, she tells us, she must 'do many bad things to live.' We've seen her eat out of trash cans, wash herself wherever she finds water, and sleep with anyone who asks her, just to get by. She tells us her spirit is wounded. I wish she would realize that she has the power to achieve a place of honor and well-being. We all give her hugs and words of encouragement when she comes to the shelter door, but we can't let her stay because she's an alcoholic. She could go to the reservation, but chooses not to." I agreed with Isabelle that losing the wisdom of Native Americans is truly a tragedy and that there must be more each one of us can do to make a difference in the lives of these people who have been stripped of so much by our culture.

With a tone of acceptance in her voice, Isabelle said, "This is my home now. The cover-up is over. At no time in my life did I ever imagine that I'd wind up living in a homeless shelter. By working here, going to various classes, and participating in church services and in life, I'm earning my way. I have to show the staff many accomplishments before I can get out on my own. When I'm ready to leave here, there are agencies and people who will help me until my government disability is approved. They will provide me with a list of available jobs, addresses, and phone numbers. St. Vincent DePaul will give me bus passes for transportation during my job search. Unfortunately, as

I've said before, many jobs here are just part-time to avoid having to provide benefits for the worker, and there is age discrimination—yes, I know it's illegal, but facts are facts. The hours are staggered at many of the work places, so it will be hard to schedule travel and establish a sleeping routine, but I'll do it. The big unknown in my life is my health and saving my leg. I'll take care of myself to the best of my ability, and that's about all I can do."

She then confided: "I have a collection of about two hundred troll dolls and many small toys. I'm taking the troll dolls with me when I leave, and later when I have the opportunity to look at them I'll have a good feeling. Even though leaving the shelter will be sad, I'll have gained something out of all this and it will keep me going. It's funny, but to me my little trolls are beautiful and make me laugh. I show them to the children who visit the shelter. What beautiful memories I have of this place. Each of my little trolls will remind me of where we've been together and how far we're going. Lord, please,... not under a bridge!" Isabelle joked.

I left with the feeling that Isabelle was one who could rise beyond her homelessness. She was, in many ways, representative of those that many shelters hope to help: those rendered homeless temporarily due to circumstances, but who, with some guidance, shelter, and assistance, can regain a place in the greater society as more fully contributing members. This will restore their self-respect and in turn give them the opportunity to help others less fortunate than they.

* * *

I called the shelter just before this book went to press and learned from the director that Isabelle's request for a government disability had been approved and that she had moved to another state. Doctors are trying to determine if an operation will save her leg.

I asked the director what trends she was seeing at the homeless shelter, and she told me that she was noticing an increase in the number of women who were mentally challenged. Some estimates claim that as much as 90 percent of homeless women are on, or should be on, medication for emotional problems; but there is inadequate funding for such medication. Another disturbing trend is that there seem to be more single middle-aged homeless women.

Julie ══════════════════════════

THE GREY-BLUE early October sky was quickly changing to a dark grey-black color, again. I wondered where the homeless women in Portland, Oregon, were taking cover during the on-again, off-again heavy rainstorms I was experiencing while in that city. It was late afternoon, and the soup kitchens and eating places for the homeless were beginning to close. The soup kitchens would probably be the last stop of the day for most of the homeless women. They would soon have to start looking for a place to spend the night. I had met with disappointment at every agency and shelter I'd gone to, because they weren't reopening for the winter until the middle of October. That meant there were no women in residence and the homeless women in the area would have to remain on the streets for another two weeks.

In spite of the setbacks, I was determined to find a homeless woman who wanted to talk to me about how she lived her life on the streets. I believed that at least one woman was out there somewhere in the city waiting to talk to me. I'd just have to find her. I decided to find a listing of the eating places that were located nearby, and, in the interest of time, decided to go to the nearest kitchen, which was called Sisters of the Road.

A homeless woman doesn't really need to worry about starving in Portland; there are at least twenty low-income meal sites equipped to serve the hungry. Some offer just coffee, cookies, and crackers; others a sack lunch; at another, a food box; and many offer complete meals for breakfast, lunch, and dinner. Any state social service office, or other organizations helping the disadvantaged, should be able to give out lists of available resources. I loved the names of these places: Chicken

Lady, Recovery Nick, Daywatch, Nightwatch, Picnic in the Park, and Sisters of the Road, the last inspiring the title of this book.

The place was packed. In addition to good food, Sisters of the Road seemed to offer spirited conversation and a chance to laugh during the hard times most of the homeless patrons were experiencing. The chattering, bustling crowd had gathered together to break bread and enjoy each other's company. It was a time when they could share their daily experiences and their dreams for a better future. I hated to interrupt them while they were eating, so I decided to speak with the manager and see if he would help me locate a homeless sister who would consent to be interviewed about her homelessness.

I met Julie a few minutes later. She was very beautiful, I thought—chestnut brown shoulder-length hair framed her face, and emerald green eyes said "hello" before she did. She wore denim jeans and a green shirt that matched her eyes. Julie was cautiously friendly and a little nervous when the manager introduced us. She seemed to me to be the "girl-next-door" type of person. Julie consented to tell me her story but said I'd have to wait for her to finish working a fifteen-minute shift that qualified her for her afternoon meal. "If a person can't work a measly fifteen minutes for their food, they deserve the painful belly. The one thing that I will complain about, though, is that the tips are lousy!" Julie laughingly told me.

After Julie finished her meal, she put on her coat and we went outside to find a place where we could sit and talk. We found a bench near a bus stop and sat down. Mother Nature was being less than cooperative, and the air smelled of rain that threatened once again. A whiff of apple cider and cinnamon emanated from a nearby foodstand, and the smell of oil from city buses was also in the air. A strange mix of scents. It was hard for Julie and I to hear each other speak above the noise of the arriving and departing buses. Deciding to find another bench where it was quieter, we huddled together under my umbrella and walked up the street. I was determined not to let the weather halt our interview.

We had just found a place to sit down when a man stopped and asked Julie if she had a cigarette she'd give him. She readily produced a cigarette, saying, "I've been there before, brother. Maybe some day you'll return the favor to someone else in need." "You're a kind lady," he said. After he left, Julie leaned back against the bench and said, "Damn, that was my last one!"

Julie began her story, announcing, "Well, it's 1995 and I'm still alive! I'll start my story where I made my first mistake. That makes sense, doesn't it? I should have finished school, but unfortunately I only attended classes through the eighth grade. I can't believe that's all the schooling I have—almost nobody makes a statement like that, or admits to it. It would have been so much easier for me just to stay in school and finish my education. I need to go back and get a GED [General Education Diploma]. I'll have to forget about the prom, I suppose. I've always known that I'll never have that memory. No ma'am, there will be no corsage for me.

"My story is pretty much the same as most other young dropouts. I left home because I wasn't getting along very well with my mom. My parents were divorced, so we only had a one-parent home. I was a latch-key kid without a key or a clue. Time after time I kept running away from home, and before long I was in trouble with the law and had to go to a detention facility. The next thing I knew I was getting married, having kids, getting divorced, getting remarried, having more kids, getting divorced again, and all before I even knew what I was doing. Finally, it hit me. I didn't know what I was doing or what I was going to do next."

This whirlwind synopsis of her life spawned more questions than it answered, but I had learned to give homeless people a free rein in telling their tales, trusting that details and clarification would come in time. If not, I could always ask questions later. This way, I didn't sidetrack trains of thought. I was also able to learn other things about the women, their personalities, and what was important to them.

Julie continued her story. "I met a guy after the break-up of my second marriage who said he'd take me away from it all. I now believe that I ran away with him because I was so overwhelmed by my responsibilities and thought I had no way to solve them. I gave my kids to their fathers. Anyway, the guy promised me that we'd travel around the country and see the beauty of the outdoors and broaden our horizons. I had no idea we'd be living outdoors on a permanent basis, learning the language of the homeless, and I'd be viewing my horizons from a park bench or from under a bridge. I traveled around several states with him and we're still friends, but both of us wonder what direction to take our relationship. We haven't been together for several months, and I think we've pretty much decided that to pursue our relationship any further would be for all the wrong reasons. One day he told me that maybe we should part company, 'especially since you're homeless and out of work right now.' A red flag went up when he made that statement to me. I interpreted it to mean that he thought I wasn't pulling my weight, not offering him enough, or he wanted me to take care of him. Anyway, the writing was on the wall and I read it. I'm learning," Julie said.

She then talked of the importance of her children and her hopes to be reunited with them. "I need to become self-sufficient and get a home before I can get my kids back. I'll do whatever's necessary to have them spend time with me. First, I'll need to get more education so I can get a good paying, respectable job. Right now I need to rely on God to take care of my children until I'm able and worthy to get them back again. I left them because I had no money, no job, no education, and no family support system. It was so traumatic and frightening for me to be left all alone and not have any idea where to get help. I don't know many people and I keep to myself—that way I don't get into trouble. I guess it's my personal style for dealing with life.

"I've slept mostly in parks during my homeless years. They are dangerous places at night because of the violent types of people staying there and the drug deals that are always going down. It isn't uncommon to watch people all around me being arrested. 'Watch out for the drug needles when you walk on the grass without your shoes!' the police officers say to me. I always have my shoes on, though, because homeless women don't dress for bed like most other women do who live in houses. I haven't had a pair of house slippers in years. Many a night, as my eyelids are closing, I wonder if they'll be opening again in the morning. The fears of the day and night have never ended for me; a melancholy seems to travel with me no matter where I go or what I do. I don't know if it's a weather-related thing or a depression from all the losses in my life. Maybe I'm just dealing with post-realization depression or something. It rains a lot of the time here in Oregon, so we usually look under bridges or for some other cover when the weather is bad. I've been terribly ill because of exposure. I keep wishing and hoping that I'll soon have a home, but sometimes I think my rainbow and pot of gold have been washed right out of the sky. I was just barely getting dry today when this rainstorm hit, and it's after three o'clock in the afternoon. It looks like another cold night for me."

Julie's struggle to retain hope was touching, and the dangers and vicissitudes of homelessness seemed especially real under the threatening skies over the beautiful city of Portland. She resumed her story without telling what brought her to this place. "When I first came to Portland, I saw an advertisement in a local newspaper for a class being taught at a nursing home. I completed the course and received a certificate as a nurse's aide, but it hasn't done me a whole lot of good. During the time I was working at the nursing home, I took a lot of time off work to go back and forth to court while filing for a divorce from my husband and seeking custody of my kids. The nursing home let me go because of my absences. I lost my job and the custody battle, too. I'm not even sure where my two oldest kids are now. I haven't heard from them since June 1993. I do know where my youngest child is, though.

"Now that I'm getting a little older and have finally figured out that a good life is like a jigsaw puzzle, I'm going to try and put the pieces back together. One big stumbling block for me is not having a permanent address, so as soon as I possibly can I'm going to get a more permanent place to stay. Most organizations can only furnish me housing for a short time, usually one week, and that isn't the answer for me. There is no way for someone to get in touch with me when I'm on the road. Even if I have people who are willing to relay a message to me, I can't call them, or an employer, because I don't have money for phone calls. 'Excuse me, do you have a quarter to spare so I can make a phone call?' I've asked people on the streets. Their reply is, 'Get a job like the rest of us!' If I'm lucky enough to get information about a job, by the time I contact the employer the job has already been filled. I also need transportation to get to an interview, and with no money for bus or cab fare it makes it difficult for me."

Clearly, being homeless presents many obtacles to overcoming that situation. Also, the rapidity with which one can become homeless swells the ranks of the homeless daily. Julie talked a bit about this. "There are so many homeless people who need help. They are all ages—young kids to elderly people in their eighties. I see them on the streets and in the kitchens every day. It's so scary. My worst nightmare is that I'll be homeless when I'm older. I need to have something to look forward to, so I visualize a nice leather purse filled with a house key, a car key, a driver's license, a little makeup, a notepad and pen, pictures of my family, a checkbook, some small change, an address book, and a handkerchief. I'd need the handkerchief to wipe away my tears of joy." Julie said wistfully.

Julie shared more of her hopes for the future, telling me, "As I've said before, I dream and visualize a lot, which I've been told is a good thing for me to do. In five years I see myself and my kids in a nice home. I cry sometimes because my house will probably never have a sandbox or playground in the backyard. My kids will be teenagers by that time. I'll have a good job, too. Sometimes when remembering what's happened to me in my life, I think, why? I then force myself to remember I was violently raped three times when I was a young teenager, all on the same night. I was classified as a runaway and was walking on the streets when I was forced into a car by a group of young guys. I was terrified and there was no one around to help me. The rapists held me down in the back seat and they all told me not to holler or there would be serious consequences. I was only thirteen years old and was traumatized beyond belief by the whole experience. The rapes blew my mind! I felt that when my body was violated my soul was murdered. I felt totally dirty and worthless. I should have had counseling but never got any. The bad choices I made after this terrible experience triggered an avalanche of troubles in my life. The path to my downfall started by choosing the wrong friends, sluffing school, going to the wrong places where the bad crowds hung out, picking up bad habits like smoking and drinking, and just plain doing the wrong things to fit in with the bad crowds.

"I now travel with a man named Michael," she revealed. "I trust him. He is a rugged, yet gentle, tall, dark, and handsome man with a good sense of humor. Not a bad combination. He is basically honest from what I've seen so far, and he's nice to me. Michael cares about his children, too, and is working toward being together with them as soon as he can. Only on the streets could I have learned so much about how this man handles basic survival in the real life struggles he faces every day. I don't know what the future holds for us. I just know that we each do what we have to do to survive, at least that is what we're doing now. I'm not making excuses for myself, just giving you the facts of my homelessness. I can't make everything better, but I can make it better than it is now.

"I'm one of the women who fall through the cracks of most government assistance programs. There are a lot of women who are alone with hardly any help. I've never been able to be all by myself on the streets, and have always had someone traveling with me," Julie then said. "My man and I were just told this week that we can get food stamps, so we applied and should be receiving them any day now. This food will free us of a lot of worry and we'll be able to concentrate on finding jobs so we can get money for a place to live. We spend a lot of time each day walking to places where we can work for our food. With more of our time available to us, we can concentrate on getting more education and jobs. Just one step at a time will get us to where we want to be.

"I have no family support system. Love has disowned me. My mother died in 1986 from heart failure, and losing her is one of my deepest sorrows. I regret the trouble I caused her and also regret not knowing her after I became an adult. I realize now that we could have been great friends. Holidays are especially hard for me to bear because I can't take back the events from the past. I treated my mom very poorly, and the words I'd most love to hear from her right now that I hated to hear years ago would be, 'Go to your room!' She'd still be here to say those words, and I'd have a room to go to. My ex-husband and I went to her home to visit on our second wedding anniversary. She apparently died about an hour after we'd left her. Mom had been ill for several years and was only forty-five years old when she died. I'm sure the problems she had with me contributed to her poor health. I'm so sorry. I mourn the truth but can't take back the trouble I caused her, no matter how much wishing and regretting I do."

She went on to tell a little about her early family life. "My biological father left us early on. He's out there somewhere living his own life with whatever woman he wants to be with at the time. As I was beginning my teenage years I found out quite by accident that my so-called 'dad' had adopted my brothers and me. Soon after learning this startling fact, my parents split up. Shortly after their divorce, my dad—I always considered him to be my real dad—called me on the telephone and told me to run away so he wouldn't have to pay child support. I perceived this to mean he didn't want to ever help me or be involved in my life," Julie said. 'Fine. See ya!' I told him. I was really born for this role.

"Several years ago I stayed with 'dear old dad' for a couple of days after getting out of a detention home. He caught me smoking a cigarette and decided to burn my hand with it. Of course I screamed and yelled really loud, so his girlfriend told him, 'Either she leaves or I leave. I'm sick of all this trouble.' To make a long story short, I left. I was only fourteen years old, but knew where I stood with him. He would always put his girlfriend's wishes above mine. I guess he loved his comfort zone too much to make waves on my behalf. He doesn't care that I'm on the streets today. I don't meet his criteria for someone whom he can be proud of, so I'm without his love. To qualify for his precious love I need to have a good education, a good track record, no bad habits, and be totally successful. I'm not perfect or good enough to suit him. Nothing I ever did seemed to make him happy."

It was obvious that this rejection had scarred Julie deeply, no doubt affecting her own concept of her self-worth and probably contributing greatly to her later troubles. I didn't understand or know the details or the exact chronological order of some of the events she mentioned, but I was able to understand the basic facts of her story and how they had affected her life. She went on to talk about her marriages and earlier life, especially the abuse she had suffered.

"My first husband physically abused me and my second husband mentally abused me. My oldest brother both physically and sexually assaulted me, beginning as early as seven years of age. Abuse, abuse, and more abuse! One afternoon my brother told me to untangle the cord on an electric recorder, but I couldn't get it undone, so he put the cord in my mouth while he untangled it, and then he plugged it in! I got an electrical charge that sent me to the hospital, and that is why I have these scars around my mouth. I've never felt pretty since getting them and have always felt self-conscious. My feelings were that because of the scars I could never get a first-class boyfriend or husband. I've always felt second-class because of the scarring, and this feeling has contributed to the type of mates and friends I've chosen throughout my life. This same brother also put me up in a tree, from which I fell to the ground and broke my arm and elbow. I guess you could say that I've always had an abundance of abusive males in my life. In fact, I never realized until recently, after counseling, that women can make conscious choices; what I used to do was just go out with whomever came along and adjust to them the best I could. Someone once told me while I was hitchhiking, 'Lady, if you go out your front door every morning and fall into a sixty-foot hole, then maybe you'd better wise up and go out your back door!' A prize has never been behind 'door number one' for me. See, I told you I have no family support system left," Julie said.

"I'm beginning to see that my needs are important and have to be met or I'll never feel that I'm worth anything," she continued. "I sometimes smile to myself and actually feel a little spoiled just acknowledging this fact. I also know that it is up to me to help myself, and I shouldn't count on a companion to solve my problems. But my companion has to be someone who wants the best for me. We'll need to have things in common and some similar goals. It would pay off for me to see him in a lot of different situations. Michael and I have been together for six months now and he's still with me. We've been through a lot. He's worked as a line cook in restaurants mostly but is now having a hard time finding work. Like I've told you, it's especially hard with no permanent address. Michael and I were staying at his brother Jake's home for a while, but we left because everybody and their dog lived there. We felt it was an unfair burden on Jake because he was struggling to keep his own family going. There were seven children, including Michael's fourteen-year-old and his six-year-old, a dog, and several adults.

"We cannot have Michael's kids living on the streets with us, so they stayed on at Jake's place. The kid's mother can't keep them, either, because she's in about the same boat as we are—floating from one motel to another when there's money, and sleeping outdoors when there is none. She works part-time tending bar; however, she seems to be a good woman in spite of her line of work. We get along fine."

Julie continued her assessment of her life. "I'm twenty-seven years old now and want to turn my life around. I was married twice before the age of twenty-one and had three kids. I failed in school, as a daughter, in marriage, as a mother; and now I'm going to make a concentrated effort to give up my old destructive patterns and habits that have caused me so much pain in my life," she vowed. She put her hand over the scars around her mouth and said, "I've always thought that when people look at me they are only seeing my scars, which probably isn't true. Some day I want to have these scars removed. I also have some medical problems that need to be checked. I'm hurting. I have constant back pain, headaches, and toothaches. In my opinion, there is no pain any worse than these pains."

I asked Julie, "If you could have one person on the streets with you, who would that person be?" She replied, "My mom. I never got along with her as a teenager, but that was my fault. The first time I ran away from home she had to go to the hospital. Eventually, she just gave up on me and agreed to sign papers for me to get married. Mom told me that I was going to do what I wanted to anyway. As I look back on this period in my life, I now realize that she was probably too ill to keep fighting the problems of raising me. After I married, my husband made me call mom more often than I had before, because there had been times when she hadn't known where I was for six months. It was so unfair of me to cause her such worry. Mom and I had started to become good friends when she was taken away from me. When I was young, I didn't realize what a parent goes through—I really didn't. Most teenagers don't realize the consequences of their actions until it's too late. If I could give young girls my best advice, it would be to look at the 'big picture.' I used to just go from day to day and not look at the big picture, and a whole lot of bad things have happened to me. I guess teenagers have the minds of kids in adult bodies. They're not good at making decisions. My mom always told me, 'Julie, anything you have to sneak to do is wrong.' That was good advice, and simple, too!"

Julie continued her assessment. "I like Portland. It isn't the town that's responsible for my homelessness. I'd have the same problems in any city. It wouldn't matter. I've got to go through the steps that I've mentioned to rebuild my life. I'm going the way of religion now. Being in church makes me feel good. It's that simple. I wish religion had been in my life when I was growing up, maybe I wouldn't have gone with the bad kids at school who sluffed and caused all sorts of trouble. I'd also believed that none of my studies were going to help me later on in my life. Now, I'm not only limited, I'm dead in the water! I still believe having my facial scars played a big part in choosing friends who had low standards, because my juvenile thoughts had told me they were all I deserved," Julie said, returning to her self-consciousness about her scars, which seemed a bit strange yet also understandable, since she was basically such a beautiful woman.

"One day I finally woke up and recognized my situation for what it was, and decided I was still young enough to change my status in life. But I don't feel young anymore. I've been through a lot," a very tired young woman lamented. "I'd like to be a nurse some day and help others. If not a nurse, something else in the medical field would be great. When I was trying to get custody of my children, the judge wanted me to get a part-time job so I could pay child support to my husband. If I'd done what the judge wanted, I would not have been able to further my education or even pay my own way. Nothing seemed to go well for me at that particular time. A lot of high school and college grads here in Portland work minimum-wage jobs. It's crazy. What chance do I have? I need experience to get a job, but I can't get the experience unless I get a job somewhere along the line," she complained. "Well, the line snapped, and I decided it was just too big a circle, or cycle, or whatever. I gave up—what doesn't go around sure can't come back around, can it?" Julie asked.

"Many days I've sat alone for hours on park benches trying to pinpoint exactly what went wrong in my life. After talking about it again today, I think I've finally narrowed it down to just two things— needing surgery to remove my scars and a stable home life when I was young. In my heart I feel that if I'd just had those two things my life would have been a lot different today. The courses I took in school should have included social and communication studies in addition to my required courses. Where was I going to get this knowledge? At home? Yeah, right. If the school system had taught me these skills and problem-solving techniques beginning in the seventh grade, I'm sure I would have made better choices. I know that now but didn't way back then. I couldn't figure anything out. It took my talks with street people and counseling to help me realize there were reasons and consequences for my actions.

"My school girlfriends hadn't known what to look for in relationships either. We didn't have a chance! We should have been more informed about poor belief systems, bad choices, con artists, bad personalities, scary psychological traits, bad manners, and addictions of all kinds. I also should have had counseling to help me work through the rapes I experienced. Help!" she exclaimed. "My list just gets longer, and, please, don't forget to teach us, as children, how to cope with abusive parents and other forms of child abuse. Not only myself, but my friends always had to put up with parents who had one bad addiction or another, or parents who were never home, or parents who hit us, or left us alone for others to abuse. We always thought everything was our fault for the crummy behavior of the adults in our lives and the terrible events that happened to us. It's really important to learn that we shouldn't waste one moment of our precious time on skunks who abuse girls and women, either mentally or physically," Julie finished, bitterly stating her complaints. No doubt much was true, but I would have felt more encouragement if she had taken more responsibility for her own situation. If nothing else, it would probably help her get out of her troubles instead of trying to be rescued from them.

"I've known some men who didn't want me to be too smart," she went on. "They told me that smart women are just too much trouble, so I've acted dumb sometimes. If women are smart, why should they try to hide it? I can see now that a smart, secure man probably wouldn't feel inferior or intimidated, but, if they do, that's their problem, isn't it? In the future I'm going to avoid anyone who doesn't respect me. I just need to find one good man. Maybe I have. If I get more education I probably won't even be attracted to poor-quality men anymore. I told you I was learning," Julie said.

Her fatalism resurfaced soon. It was hard for her not to see herself as a loser and her life as already wasted. "By the time I'd figured out a lot of things, I'd already destroyed my chances for a good life. Now, I have to live with the consequences. Someone on the streets told me that the ripple effect doesn't finish rippling for seven generations. Ouch! And I thought these benches were hard! I don't like being alone, but I'm afraid to trust people because of the hurt they've caused me in the past. If I can just be around them … they don't even have to say any-thing to me, just be there and I'll be fine," Julie said, as she finished our interview and returned to the streets. All I could do was hope that she would find someone to encourage her and that luck and good fortune would come to her side for a change.

Sarah ═══════════════════

HOMELESSNESS in one sense can be the fate of some people who actually have physical shelter and nominal support but who have been bullied or otherwise made to feel so insecure as to psychologically be homeless. Sometimes this situation can lead to actual homelessness, and, for all its attendant sorrow and heartache, perhaps in some ways those people are the luckier ones—particularly if they then can find someone to help them get out of the resultant homeless situation. I met a woman named Sarah who was in this predicament, although it seemed to be partly of her own making, or at least acceptance. I want to briefly tell her story because it shows a connection between abuse and homelessness, because Sarah was in some sense physically homeless for periods, and because it may help other abused women take the risk of leaving their abusive partners or situations ... even at the risk of homelessness. On the streets, at least, one can seek help.

Sarah was a patient at a hospital in southeastern Ohio. I was there waiting for a member of a group I was with to receive treatment for an injury. Sarah was sitting on a bench in the garden area and appeared to be upset. I hoped that maybe I could help calm her. After our introductions, she told me that she was going to be released from the hospital later in the day. She said her daughter and son-in-law were coming to pick her up and were taking her to their home, because she couldn't return to the house she shared with her husband.

I wondered what she meant when she said that she could not return to her own house. "Where's your home?" I asked.

"I've lived most of my life in an Amish religious community in the state," she answered. "I have a deep sense of my heritage and believe that life is a homeward journey back to God and my loved ones. I feel that time will soon be here for me. I'm quite sure this will be my last trip to a hospital in the outside world. I'm trying to pass away with courage and be dignified about it all—telling myself that everyone comes into this world alone and we all must leave the same way. I count my blessings daily, and that seems to help me," Sarah said sadly. At that point she lost her battle to hold back the tears.

I took Sarah's hand and held it for a few minutes. "Your history sounds very interesting, Sarah, do you feel well enough to share more of it with me?" I finally asked, being both curious and hopeful that talking about her situation might lessen her anxiety.

Sarah pondered for a moment, then began. "I've lived in our community with my husband, Jacob, for many years and have been shunned in varying degrees during our entire marriage. It has been necessary for me to travel to the 'English world' many times to get the medical help I've needed, but Jacob doesn't want any part of it." The "English" Sarah referred to was the outside world in general, those outside the Amish community. She continued. "When I wake up here at the hospital each morning, a cheerful nurse says, 'Good morning, Sarah!' This is a very different greeting from the one I receive from Jacob each morning. He always asks me, 'Are you ready for the bone yard?'"

Sarah confided that she felt worthless because she had never been able to stand up to Jacob and demand her rights as a human being. She had been paralyzed by his verbal abuse and rigid control since they met. "You're wondering why I put up with his abuse. I'm weak, I guess," Sarah murmured. "I'm so upset now, because I feel that I don't belong anywhere. My children have all left home and have their own lives, and Jacob never says anything of value to me and has instructed me to go elsewhere to die. I live a very sad and lonely existence. No one in my community, including my family, are supposed to speak to me, eat with me, or show any sign of recognition when they see me. I'm an outcast and I'm sick. This shunning is especially painful for me to endure at this time. I'm as good as dead in everyone's eyes."

Before I could think of anything meaningful to say, she resumed: "I've completely worn myself out taking care of everyone else. Before coming to this hospital I thought I might be dying and said, 'Jacob, please stay home today from your church meeting. I really need you to be here.' His words hurt deeply: 'Sarah, you're just a dead horse that won't lay down. I'm not going to waste my time or money on someone who will just end up at the glue factory! You have no purpose here. You cannot bear me any more children; you're too old to hook up to a plow;… you're no longer a woman. Don't try to divorce me either; you won't get any money from me and then you'll just be homeless again and starve. You work for the devil, you do … trying to get me to stay home from church! Why don't you go elsewhere to die?'"

Sarah commenced to answer my unspoken question about how she had ended up with her husband. It was evident that she had soon regretted her marriage to him. "He'd noticed me at church and started the courting ritual. I was twenty-five years old and he was forty-one. I noticed pompous and pious traits in his demeanor. Being an unmarried woman at twenty-five was very uncommon in our community, so I'm sure he thought he was doing me a favor by rescuing me from spinsterhood.… He loves the power and feeling of control he has over others. It could be a truly happy way of life if our men were sincere in their commitment to love God and their families as the Bible teaches. The pleasant life God promised for being faithful has never materialized for me or our family because of Jacob's misuse of power.

"We women take a vow when we marry to conform to the teachings of our church and to the wishes of our husbands. I've labored hard because of love for God and my family.… After working hard all my life the only important possessions I have to show for my labor are my nine wonderful children (six are living), and my friendships. I don't seem to have a home." She said that Jacob told her to leave many times, and that for extended periods of time she stayed with her children. "He says he doesn't want me to return, but I return anyway."

She told a bit about her life. "After finishing school at the end of the tenth grade it was back to the farm for me. This was considered to be a long education for a girl in our community. Most girls only attend school through the eighth grade, because too much schooling might lead to a feeling of self-importance.

"I loved making quilts and attending quilting bees.… It was important to me to please my mother and find a bigger place in her heart, so I did my best to learn the crafts. With the exception of my mother, most of my family only laughed when my quilts were finished. They hurt my feelings beyond belief. As a child, many of my hours were spent alone, dreaming of the day I'd be accepted and loved. Being alone most of the time caused me to become somewhat distant. I was always trying to please others. Measuring up to the expectations of my family seemed to be impossible for me, and I didn't really know why. What did my heart want? Unconditional love and acceptance, maybe. Now, I'm afraid my extreme humility has been used against me ever since.

"Being shy and socially backward were definite drawbacks for me when it came to choosing a mate. There had only been one gentleman caller in my life other than Jacob, and he'd moved away. I often wondered if he still thinks about me, too. Unmarried women in our community pursued careers, usually in teaching, art, medicine, or some service-related field. They usually live with their family and help raise their nieces and nephews to fill their motherly instincts," she revealed.

"Jacob has controlled me from the first day I met him," she claimed. She said that their courtship was dreary; but she then revealed that she had become pregnant by him out of wedlock, although she claimed that he had manipulated her into sexual activity as well. It was becoming clear that she may have allowed others to take advantage of her but that she was not very willing to take responsibility for her actions.

"Jacob blamed me for everything that had happened, saying, 'You tempted me and led me to sin! You've broken the commandments and will be an outcast because of what you've caused the both of us!' I can truthfully say that I was not the initiator nor the instigator of the act. Shame consumed me . . . I was void of any hope. I felt no love or joy toward this man. Jacob told me, 'You will pay dearly for the embarrassment you've caused me!' But then, he added, 'However, I'm willing to do the right thing and marry you.'

"I felt sorry for myself and my baby and was uncertain of what lay ahead.... I finally found the courage to tell my parents. But, as a result, my family all treated me differently. I was like a bad seed. Everyone except my mother acted coldly and reserved toward me. She only hurt for me. My secret was one that couldn't be kept from our community for very long.... Out of sheer desperation, I decided to run away. Jacob must have seen me leave home, because he caught up with me and shouted, 'You're not going to take my child away from me! My child will live under my roof! I have my rights. The Lord's words and my words are one and the same! We will raise up the child in the church, but it won't be in this community.'

"Jacob told me, 'You must leave your family here, both in body and in memory and come with me. You have shamed me and you have shamed them!' I was exhausted and thought 'only atonement will save me from my pain.' To this day, I cannot bear to speak about our wedding day. I left my spirit at my parent's front door as Jacob and I left to begin our life together. I hid pictures of my family in an old box of hair pins. No one had rescued me from my mistake as I'd hoped they would.

"Jacob pretended to be a good, godfearing man in our new community. I cried most of the time until the birth of my baby. I was so lonesome without my family and friends.... Finally, I decided to try to forget about the things I couldn't change and make the best of my situation for my child's sake. But Jacob constantly droned on and on about my shame."

I had told Sarah that I planned to write a book on homeless women, and she assumed that there would be a chapter devoted to her and went on to say, "I'm sure many members of my family and the public will believe that since I've done nothing about the abuse, then I deserve what I'm getting. I'm sorry for going on and on with my tales of woe, but I've stayed in the marriage for several reasons: I must obey the laws of God and our church, I must always mind my husband and take care of him, and I believe divorce is evil. In the early years of our union, I considered leaving many times, though I was taught that it was not an option. I never did, though, mostly because I was afraid that I couldn't support the children and myself. I decided in later years that I was going to endure to the end because of my religion, but I couldn't believe that this marriage, and the hell I'd lived through, was God's will," Sarah said, in justifying remaining in her marriage.

Sarah's eyes showed happiness as she told me about the birth of her first child. "When my baby was born, it was like the baby only belonged to God and me. Other children were born to me later and they were also loved dearly. Jacob hadn't embraced all of the shunning practices and slept with me as a wife. My children seemed quite happy in our home, probably because in our community our good friends and neighbors visited us daily and the children were always at ease around them. They were never at ease when alone with their father and had to act like jesters to get him to be pleasant or smile. Jacob had to be on his best behavior when others were around, though, or word might have gotten out. The children were hard workers. They were not spoiled. The time we all liked best was when Jacob was gone from the house. He was always either in the fields or doing his church work."

Talking seemed to be doing Sarah good. Her assessment of Jacob, her children, and her life had animated her. The thought that her tale might be appearing in a book had loosened her tongue, although I believe that many readers will believe that she exaggerated her husband's villany, particularly since she had nine children by him and they did not see him exactly as she did. She went on: "Being a mother is my greatest reward. Keeping my home clean, my garden beautiful, and good food on the table were always very important to me. I tried to compensate for Jacob's nastiness by making our family life as happy as I could. I'm thankful that I had the strength at that time in my life to carry out these very important tasks. My children kept me going through some unbearable times. Year after year I remained isolated from my family during the dinner hour and ate on a folding table in a corner. To this day Jacob still says I'm not worthy to join him at his table. Jacob told me that when the children were old enough to understand he was going to tell them about me getting pregnant before our marriage. I worried myself sick about it when I was younger, but I finally decided there was nothing I could do about the things he said."

I was a bit bewildered and couldn't understand how he could be thought blameless in the matter of her first pregnancy, but I resolved to let her tell her story, in hopes clarity would come.

"My husband told me to leave his home many times, especially when I became ill and couldn't work, couldn't wait on him, or if I cost him money. Around the house I could not open my mouth before he rudely and contemptuously told me to 'be quiet.' Jacob eats alone at his table now that the children have all gone. When his meal is finished, he gets up and retreats to a church meeting, to the fields, or to the basement, where he reads scriptures or goes over other plans. He doesn't speak to me. What is he thinking about … or is he brooding? I've never known. Why has he always been so unhappy? Has it been because of our sexual sin so long ago? I believe the Bible, and Jacob supposedly does too, so why doesn't he believe in forgiveness?" Sarah asked.

"For years I kept hoping that Jacob would change, but it hasn't happened and I don't suppose it ever will. He has always demeaned me in front of the children and referred to me as a 'dirty old thing.' … If word ever got out to the men in our community about Jacob's mistreatment of his family, they ignored it."

Her recitation of old hurts was beginning to seem neverending, but I resolved to hear her out (although I've omitted much here) since it was just a pale reflection of the pain she must have endured living through them. She even mentioned that her husband talked of getting another wife and had entered into negotiations with a marriage broker. It was not clear if he thought he could then just dump Sarah aside. The two of them definitely had a strange relationship.

She sat motionlessly for several moments, and then said, "As soon as each child was old enough to be on their own, they left our home. I understood, but without my children the house was a very lonely place. Two children even left our community. When our daughter Jane left home to marry someone from the outside world Jacob disowned her. He said, 'You're going straight to hell!' I said nothing. I'm very ashamed of myself for this act of cowardice. I am acutely aware that I failed my child by remaining silent in the matter.

"Jacob loved to preach…. He told me over and over again, 'Those doctors are just quacks and want my money. I can heal you—me and the Lord!' Jacob's healing has only made me worse," Sarah said. She then began a recitation of her health woes and problems that developed with her husband because of them and their expense, even speculating that he purposely withheld medication from her.

I began to suspect that Sarah found some satisfaction in her own submissiveness, for she continually stressed it and her weakness. Despite her claim of homelessness and wish to be included in the book, her words revealed how desperate she was to avoid actual homelessness: "Can you imagine a woman being so submissive that she would allow herself to be controlled to the point of risking her life? I wasn't worthy, in Jacob's eyes, to receive any benefits for all my years of work and service to the family. There was no love. I'm still trying to please him, can you imagine? I just want to live out my last days in the little house where I've worked so hard and raised my children. I haven't been able to have any freedom of my own or to visit my relatives…. My children have had to worry about me, which they shouldn't have had to do. I suspect my family really doesn't respect me, and I can surely understand if this is the case," she acknowledged, but maintained, "It wasn't all my fault. I'm sure I'm not alone in my feelings against the form of humility our women must practice.

"As I've mentioned, Jacob doesn't want me, so my children take turns keeping me. Then it occurred to me on this bench that I have a home and should have the right to return there, no matter what consequences I must face. I've worked hard my entire life for it and deserve its comfort now that I'm dying. It will be hard for me to beg and humble myself and be subjected to the insults of Jacob when I return.

I know that it will cause me a great deal of stress, but I don't like being a burden on my children. I don't feel comfortable to be ill in the home of others. It's a terrible feeling to be homeless and have to impose on others for a place to stay," Sarah said with tears in her eyes. "Ladies, be very careful when you marry, it might be your life," Sarah warned, changing the topic slightly to address her hoped-for audience.

Sarah was a timid person who tried to be so selfless that she lost much that was best in life, including a true home. As such, I believe her story should be included in this book on homelessness. I also believe that an expanded definition of homelessness may be beneficial to many. Therefore I am including excerpts from Sarah's long tale of abuse, although I also believe that she used the situation to stress the pathetic aspects of her life. This could be seen in lines of some poetry that she had written and shared with me: "Eyes so dim I could barely see, to thread a needle, poor blind me. Each loving stitch was placed with care, they were uneven, but just left there." After reciting her poem, Sarah said, "I hope the Lord will forgive me for wondering if dying wouldn't be better for me and my family. I don't want to be a burden, and living in a body full of pain is very draining and depressing. I feel there really isn't any reason for me to go on. I just don't believe I'm worth much any more and realize there isn't much left of me."

Pondering the quality of her life, Sarah said: "I'm homeless, even though I have a husband who seems to have a home. He's told me over and over again to leave, and I do. I've never really known what legal arrangements Jacob has regarding the land we live on. He's never discussed any financial matters with me. I've always been kept in the dark about money. He's told me more than once, 'This house is mine. You will abide by, and not question, my business or my orders.' I'm sorry that I've succumbed to an oppression that has left me without a home and no means to provide for myself in times of trouble and old age. I was irresponsible and cowardly, and have now ended up with nothing. I'll have to worry and beg for my every need for what's left of my life." With downcast eyes, Sarah said, "I let him destroy me."

* * *

After returning home I contacted social service agencies in her state and obtained information that would help Sarah. I wrote, hoping to hear from her soon; however, no letter or call came. After waiting two weeks, I called her daughter Ruth. I was saddened but not surprised when Ruth told me that Sarah had decided to return to her house and accept whatever awaited her. Ruth continued, "My brothers and sisters also tried to persuade mother to stay with them, but she declined. I now believe she was letting go of her struggle to survive."

Ruth sorrowfully went on. "I'm afraid this isn't the worst of my news. Mother passed away last week. It's painful for me to speak about my mother and father, but mother told me she'd enjoyed meeting you, and hoped that by sharing her story she might help young women make better choices in selecting a partner.... I don't have good feelings about my father's treatment of my mother," Ruth said bitterly.

"Mother's best friend was a woman named Mary. She told me that she and some of the other church sisters went to visit mother the day before she died. Mother was in her bedroom, sitting on the floor rocking back and forth, half crying, half singing, in a weak voice: 'I'm forever blowing bubbles, pretty bubbles in the air.' I was not surprised mother was singing this song, it was her favorite," Ruth said. Recalling the song's lines about dreams fading, I wasn't surprised either; but I definitely was shocked when Ruth said that before she died Sarah had literally crawled to where Jacob was working and asked to be buried by his side. He hadn't even answered her, Ruth reported.

She continued, "The sisters were dumbfounded by mother's encounter with father. Mary told me she had no idea of the depth of my father's cruelty. Mother told her, 'Mary, I'm not complaining, but sometimes it just helps to talk to someone. I count my blessings.... Maybe the agony will soon be over for me.... I've turned everything over to God. I returned to this house because I wanted to die in my own room. God help me, and God help Jacob, too."

I offered my sincere condolences to Ruth and her family. Even though Jacob had badly mistreated her, Sarah never really spoke ill of him to her children. She wanted her story told in an effort to save others from making the mistakes she made. She wanted girls to be aware of the pitfalls they will face if they choose the wrong mate, and that the regret could last their lifetime. I remember Sarah telling me, "I've waged such a battle to keep up appearances, and have basically given up my life to make everyone in my family happy. My belief was that sweet rewards awaited me if I kept the commandments in the Bible. I made sure everyone was properly taken care of and going down the right path, but I didn't carve out much of a path for myself."

Epilogue

AT THE END OF THIS BOOK, I want to reiterate that these stories about women who ended up homeless are true, although most of the stories have been edited and/or paraphrased in some places. Most of the women asked for help. Some didn't. A few didn't care whether their stories saved other women from making the same mistakes they had made. Others cared very much, and many hoped that telling their stories would help other women save themselves great suffering and personal loss.

The interviews were both painful and rewarding to me. Tears of sadness and joy were shed by the homeless women and myself. There was laughter as we told stories back and forth about the many stupid mistakes we'd made in our lives. As Virginia Woolf wrote: "If you do not tell the truth about yourself, you cannot tell it about other people."

Homelessness is most commonly the physical condition of not having a permanent shelter of one's own. We have seen, however, that some women like Sarah may technically have such a shelter but can still be considered virtually homeless because of its unpleasantness or threat to them. Actual physical homelessness might even conceivably be a better situation for them. Others, like Dominique, seem to be able to adapt to the circumstance of being without a regular home by making a "home" out of temporary quarters. Some natural vagabonds or adventurers actually like living as homeless beings. I remember one little lady about sixty-five-years old who asked me, "Can you tell me what the secret is for ending my homelessness? Well, if you know, just whisper it in my ear and I won't listen." And she got up and walked down the street! I'll bet she's still on the streets. She liked the lifestyle.

Homelessness is a dangerous lifestyle, however—one to be embraced by very few. Many stay in it for long periods because they will not or do not know how to take the steps to rise from it. This is a tragedy, made even more sad if children are adversely affected by such conditions. Most homeless people, I believe, would like to have permanent homes and a more stable life. It is they that I would like this book to help as it also endeavors to help others avoid the slippery slope of homelessness that is so easy for most of us to fall into.

It is a painful realization to become aware that each of us could be on the streets if one or more unexpected occurrences were set into play. Studies have shown that a surprisingly high percentage of people are only two paychecks away from the streets. When a person has no support system, such as family, friends, or a group of some kind, homelessness can result. Do you feel lucky? Will your physical and mental health hold up if you are without help? Have you enough savings to live on until you find another job? Will you lose your house? Your car? Your insurance? Your meal ticket? You are advised to ask yourself these questions and then to take remedial action to change the situation if you don't like the answers.

To my mind, being homeless is somewhat like being a lost, forgotten camper alone in a dangerous area with no provisions for survival, and little chance of rescue—unable to return to the comforts of home. It can be a trip that is neverending unless the tools for rescue and change are found and used.

Being mired in bad situations and bad places doesn't have to be a permanent way of life for homeless women. When a woman has a crisis of any kind that seems to be impossible for her to work through, prompt intervention and counseling from a reputable source can make the difference between recovery and disaster. For various reasons, many people don't know how to work their way out of trouble or where to find the kind of help they need. Some travel on "automatic pilot," doing what they consider to be their best to survive, but generally reacting to events that happen to them rather than taking conscious directed or willful action with some defined goal or plan in mind.

There are women without a home that either don't see, or refuse to see, that they are the cause of many of their tragedies. Sometime, somehow, somewhere, we, as fellow human beings, must find a way to help such homeless women help themselves. If each of us, individually or in groups, would just find one homeless woman, and concentrate our best efforts toward her recovery, what a difference there would be in our society.

In many of the stories I have included in this book, women without homes believed they didn't have the power or control in their lives to make the changes necessary to improve their situations. Most felt helpless but actually were not. Unable to recognize their own situations for what they are, perhaps lost in the victim cycle, afraid to take any kind of action because it might be a wrong move, submitting to the will of others either on or off the streets, or worrying about whether or not they will offend others if they stand up for themselves are among the self-imposed patterns that can lead women to their worst fears. Drugs and alcohol play a major role in some of the stories, as does physical abuse. Suffering and turmoil will remain in their lives if positive changes are not made.

Dramatic changes can be made in the lives of women who learn and apply lessons from counseling and intervention. Letting bad things happen without protest or struggle is destructive. In their stories, one could identify where mistakes were made that contributed to their problems and homelessness. A reader who questions herself as to what she might do differently if confronting the same set of circumstances could learn much and would at least be reminded how vulnerable she might be to homelessness.

With the help of professional counselors and social workers, I have prepared a list of some of the qualities or traits of women that can lead them into difficulties that could well end in their own homelessness. It would hopefully benefit many women if they would use it to candidly assess themselves and their situation. As mentioned in the Introduction, I call such prime candidates for homelessness selfless women.

Selfless Women:
•Do not accept responsibility for their lives, if capable.
•Give up their power.
•Do not give up their
    Roles as martyrs or victims,
    Bad habits and addictions,
    Destructive patterns,
    Old fears, guilt, worry, and hurts.
•Refuse to believe that they can do something about their
    homelessness.

•Postpone their education, counseling, and rehabilitation.
•Are not assertive enough.
•Do not reach out to others for help.
•Set limits upon themselves.
•Do not take steps to ensure their financial position and security.
•Have greater than normal capacity for…

> Accepting the duties and responsibilities of others,
> Accepting misplaced blame, unjust criticism, insults, and demeaning remarks,
> Accepting problems of others as their own,
> Being a doormat or at the mercy of others,
> Being taken for granted or excluded,
> Feeling inadequate,
> Getting into a bind,
> Going around in circles,
> Sacrifice, self-denial, self-punishment,
> Squashing their own desires, except the one to please,
> Staying in limbo,
> Putting their own needs last.

How can homeless women, or those whose lifestyle or conditions may soon lead to homelessness, pull themselves out of this lifeway? It won't be easy and will involve great effort and desire on their part. The homeless women of our country also need the help of others—you and me—to find a new life. I want to make a difference for such women, and I believe that the information media in this country can help. I want to help expose some of the problems and then propose specific solutions to help women avoid homelessness. Americans believe in helping others. We seize hope and initiative; we are optimistic. Homelessness is a terrible problem, but it is one we can all help solve.

I wrote this book as one way of taking a step in making others aware of this terrible problem. As Janice Kapp Perry wrote in her song "The Least of These": "Give me a heart that sees another's need, And love to share with the least of these…. The measure of a life is what we share, How we care about God's hurting children everywhere."

I believe that if there is enough information and understanding available to women who are homeless then perhaps asking for and receiving the help they need will become as natural to them as going to a doctor when they have an illness.

If the government, churches, private agencies, and charities really want to end homelessness, sufficient funds should be provided for good intervention and outreach programs that can transform lives. Programs are out there that will work if participants are capable and sincerely want change, but they need adequate funding to effectively reach and then treat those homeless people on the street.

There are some things that can be done to help women from becoming homeless. As parents, we can stop grooming our daughters for failure. Give them good schooling and the tools that will sustain them throughout their lives. Give them positive words that will help mold their attitudes and personalities, filling their minds with love and a sense of worth. Help every girl find a sense of self early in her life. Let girls explore. Don't set your girls up for failure by not providing an escape route; see that they have the skills to survive on their own. Teach both boys and girls to be giving. Teach your boys to nurture, too. Instill in the minds of young men that while out "sowing their wild oats" they must not destroy the lives of young women. Don't practice or tolerate abuse of any kind in your home, for it very likely will manifest itself later in the lives of your children. This is about equality. Teach good values and spiritual principles to all children and provide all with equal opportunity and encouragement to try to be whatever they wish to be.

Girls must also help themselves. Don't follow the crowds that encourage anything inappropriate, such as drug and alcohol use, immorality, disrespect for others, and other temptations that might destroy you. These groups include those who encourage you to sluff school and neglect your studies, thus preventing you from obtaining the education you will need to ensure a better future for yourself and your posterity. Don't give yourself away . . . give yourself a chance. Be true to yourself. You are unique. You are special, just the way you are. Don't dumb yourself down. Don't feel you're not "measuring up" to the models and actresses. Don't diet until you disappear. If the truth was known, the models and actresses probably don't "measure up" to you. Learn to entertain yourself. Don't be spoiled or a "high maintenance" type of individual. Learn about values.

Women who are already homeless need to get out of the loop and exit the maze of homelessness. Focus on the big picture—a future that will take you to a place of security. Get the help you need, now! Enroll in programs that will help you at your local shelters, schools, churches,

YWCA, Salvation Army, charities,and state and federal social services agencies. Women's homeless shelters are great places to gather yourself, protect yourself, and rest and heal yourself. Keep active and keep your mind active. Expand it, too! Don't cave-in to bad habits and procrastination. Kick the bad habits with professional help. Don't lose yourself searching for help from someone who is in worse shape than you are! Life is very precious … don't waste another minute of it. Learn to trust the professional people.

It is my opinion that the most important thing a person can do if they find themselves in dire need and homeless is to fight the particular circumstance with all their might! Doing nothing to improve the situation is inviting yourself on the lonely journey of homelessness. Let me say it again: Keep active. Keep your mind active! It is truly a matter of choosing to change your perceptions and enter into the reality that there is help for you. Go immediately to a social services office in your city or county and find out what programs are available to help you. Go to local churches and charity organizations. Look in the yellow pages for help for your particular problem. Help can be found in many places. Remember, every human being needs help at some point in their lifetime. The danger is in doing nothing and becoming too caught up in a homeless lifestyle and settling into it. If a woman becomes ill, or has no energy or desire to change her circumstance, she will very likely become immobilized by fear, depression, or apathy. The programs available can provide help to women who want to make the necessary changes to cease being homeless.

All Americans should challenge themselves to help our homeless sisters and brothers immediately! You have the opportunity to help them with their burdens and to help the charities and churches who are also struggling to provide for them. By organizing as volunteer groups, or even on our own, perhaps we can break through the personal problems and patterns of the homeless and alleviate their plight. The shelters are a homeless person's first line of defense. Please give generously to them. Call or visit a shelter today and see what they need. If they don't get donations that are critically needed, they can't provide them to the homeless. Share your talents, your harvest, and especially your teaching skills and the tools and materials to complete various projects.

Shop for food, clothing, books, learning tools, supplies, and toys for those less fortunate. If you see someone eating out of a garbage can, give them a sack lunch! Distribute lunches. Take some fruit or bottles of juice, a blanket, a pillow, a smile, a hug, and a word of hope. Spirits will soar and you will feel the joy that comes from giving. Personally, or as a group or couple, adopt a homeless sister.

Take a walk on the wild side—visit the heart of the city. Forget about meeting that well-groomed person for lunch who endlessly chats about his or her wants. Instead, the two of you can have lunch with a homeless woman and have a heart-to-heart talk with her about how to get her off the streets. Ask yourself what you can do to give her strength and knowledge that will help her in her effort to become self-sufficient. What can you teach her? It could be fun and will be satisfying. There are children and elderly tenants at the shelters and rescue missions who require special items, such as medical supplies, formulas, and diapers. Furniture and bedding are also needed at the shelters. There are many ways we can help. Be a big brother or sister to a homeless youngster. Teach them a skill, share a hobby, or take them on an outing. Many of them cannot read or write well—help them. Teach them to paint, or sew, or to use a computer. Teach them to play the piano or guitar. Take them to a movie, a ball game, or to the zoo.

Unfortunately, it is true that there is danger in some areas, so take precautions, including asking a friend or family member to go with you for safety and support. Call the shelter and ask for directions and assistance before you go. Be aware of the surroundings and check out the area for possible trouble before going in. After you enter the shelter, you most likely will immediately see many things you can do to help. Your heart may soften; tears may flow. Your character will grow. You'll feel better about yourself than if you'd just spent two weeks at some posh luxury retreat or resort. Come on … get started!

My wish for each woman is to follow her chosen path to a fulfilling life. If lessons can be learned from the experiences of our "sisters of the road," then it would be wise to learn from them and avoid the roads leading to heartbreak, loneliness, poverty, danger, emptiness, and just plain misery. After interviewing women who have been homeless, I found out that when they have eliminated substance abuse, taken care of their medical problems, had counseling relative to their psychological problems, accepted themselves fully, learned a skill, found meaningful work, and/or attended a church of their choice on a regular basis their lives improved dramatically.

As women, knowing the dangers in human relationships, we must do everything in our power to become more knowledgeable and understanding of them and become more self-sufficient and stronger in order that we can take care of ourselves and others we love if the need arises. We are limited, for the most part, by our health, our knowledge, our financial position, our energy, our imaginations (or lack thereof), our values, and our fears. I've found that most women who make positive lifestyle changes enjoy better health, have more energy, are happier in their relationships with others, have stronger families, and their fears diminish considerably. What can each of us do that will make a difference? Take that first step … begin. The actions you take are the ones that count and will get you to your goal, whether it's a better life for yourself or a helping hand for a homeless "sister of the road." Lines from a song by James Marsden and Thurl Bailey have moved me, and I would like to close this book with them in the hope that they will also inspire others.

> He saw her standing on the corner
> With her hand stretched out
> To take anyone's dime
> She had a baby in the other arm
> And a little boy by her side
> He didn't care about the dirt on her face
> Or the ragged dress that she wore
> He could see the cry from the woman inside
> 'Cause he'd been there before.
> It doesn't matter where she came from
> It doesn't matter how she got that way
> It doesn't matter if she's black or white
> When it's love that saves the day
> When you're looking through the eyes of love
> Past appearance to the heart and soul
> You might see an angel behind those eyes
> When your love saves the day.

ORDER FORM

Please ask for this book at your local bookstore. You also can use this page (or a copy of it) to order.

Please send me ___ copy(ies) of *Sisters of the Road.* I am enclosing $17.95 for each copy (plus $3.50 to cover postage and handling). Send check, money order, or credit card information, no cash or C.O.D.s.

Name:_____

Address: _____

City/State/Zip: _____

Please charge my: ___ Visa; ___ MasterCard; ___ Discover;
    ___ Other (please identify) _____

Card Account No._____
    Exp. Date:_____

Signature of Card Holder: _____

    Number of copies: _____ @ $17.95 each:_____.

    Shipping and handling: $3.50.

    (Utah residents please add 5.75% sales tax: _____.

    Total amount enclosed: _____.

Send order to: Pine Canyon Press, 2151 East Pine Canyon Road, Lincoln, Utah 84074.

Call your credit card order to: Toll free 1-888-404-3188; or fax to 1-435-882-3188. Please allow two to three weeks for delivery.

A portion of the proceeds from this book will be donated to shelters for homeless women.